Illinois Architecture

This guide to Illinois architecture was published under the auspices of the Illinois Sesquicentennial Commission, which was created by the Illinois 74th and 75th General Assemblies and signed into law by Governor Otto Kerner for the purpose of "investigating the most effective, suitable and appropriate means for commemorating the 150th anniversary of the admission of the State to the Union." Chairman of the Commission was Ralph G. Newman. Chief of Arts Program was Helen Tieken Geraghty. The Architectural Committee appointed by the Commission responsible for initiating this project consisted of the following: Jack H. Swing, Chairman of the Department of Architecture, University of Illinois, Urbana; George E. Danforth, F.A.I.A., Head of the Department of Architecture and City Planning, Illinois Institute of Technology; Donald D. Hanson, Chairman of the Department of Architecture, University of Illinois, Chicago Circle; Earl W. Henderson, Springfield, Central Illinois Chapter, A.I.A.; Edgar E. Lundeen, Bloomington, Central Illinois Chapter, A.I.A.; and Earl H. Reed, F.A.I.A. Advice and encouragement also came from John Entenza, Director of the Graham Foundation for Advanced Studies in the Fine Arts, and George M. Irwin, Chairman of the Illinois Arts Council.

Frederick Koeper

Illinois Architecture

From Territorial Times to the Present
A Selective Guide

The University of Chicago Press
Chicago and London

Dedicated to the memory of
Earl H. Reed, 1884–1968
Fellow of the
American Institute of Architects

International Standard Book Number: 0–226–44993–9
Library of Congress Catalog Card Number: 68–16700

The University of Chicago Press, Chicago 60637
The University of Chicago Press, Ltd., London

Foreword

One hundred and fifty years ago few trails crossed
this rich land that was to become the twenty-first
state. Yet where those few trails crossed, and
the early pioneers settled, began the growth that
transformed the then remote western plain into the
vital and influential state it is today.

In this sesquicentennial year the story of growth of
this great state is being re-examined and
re-expressed, and this survey of significant Illinois
architecture is an examination of buildings that
contributed to, and have left their mark upon, the
growth of our state—buildings that tell the story of
the strength and dignity, ingenuity and craftsmanship, ambitions and vitality of her people.

To select one hundred and fifty buildings of
significance is no small task. The selection began
with generally accepted historical examples, but it
was soon apparent that there was a much longer list
representing different periods of architecture,
various architectural concepts, masterpieces of
craftsmanship, innovations of construction, and
works of great and renowned architects. Also the
types of structures that might be represented
expanded the list. Should not the covered bridge,
which played such an important part in the days of
the horse and buggy, stand side by side with the
great and busy air terminals of this day? Should not
the comfortable homes, which sit way back in
the shade of giant trees, tell their story of another
day, as the skyscraper and the high-rise apartment
make their contribution to modern Illinois?

To see a building, a road, a stained-glass window, a
park, or a complex of buildings is to see at the same
time a statement of the economic and social condi-
tions, artistic sensitivity, materials and methods of

construction, and ways of life that express the ambitions and rewards of generations. Though a building
may have endured a major change in surroundings
and though its use may have altered, its contribution
to history and to the community remains significant
and a record for future generations.

In conclusion, it was agreed that this survey of the
richness of Illinois architecture should record
the vitality of the present as well as summarize the
long history of the state. We are a mobile people;
we live in high buildings; we travel in various
ways. Our buildings and cities are a measure of
contemporary civilization. The panorama of life
today is composed in part of unusual buildings
which range from factory complexes to giant
arenas for sporting events. At the edge of the
sparkling waters of Lake Michigan significant new
structures have been strategically placed—such as
the observatory at Northwestern University—
constructed to serve a purpose as surely as the old
Fort de Chartres overlooking the waters of the
Mississippi served its purpose. Thus this book is a
record of both the past and present.

It is the hope of the Architectural Committee that
this book will serve as a guide to Illinois and its
heritage. Each of these one hundred and fifty
buildings and structures adds a measure to our
understanding of the growth of Illinois. Illinois is a
state of many accomplishments and with a proud
history. Its architecture is a substantial share of that
history and those accomplishments.

Earl W. Henderson, Jr.
Architect, A.I.A.
Springfield, Illinois

Preface

There is no state in the union whose history of architecture can match in total importance that of Illinois. The retrospective of Illinois architecture is impressive and varied—although admittedly individual styles and architects may be better represented elsewhere. The Virginia colony yielded the richest Georgian, and later the work of Thomas Jefferson. New York has superb examples of Greek Revival, as well as the polished work of McKim, Mead and White. Massachusetts can claim examples by Peter Harrison and Henry Hobson Richardson. Yet none of these states can, in their historical entirety, present a comparable history of significant architectural achievement. Illinois understandably did not produce much in the eighteenth century. But for the nineteenth and twentieth centuries, it presents a representative variety of architectural styles, innovations of world-wide import, and the heartland of Louis Sullivan, Frank Lloyd Wright, and Ludwig Mies van der Rohe. Chicago has long been recognized throughout the world as the city that gave birth to modern architecture. It is therefore appropriate to the sesquicentennial year of the state of Illinois that its architectural heritage be reaffirmed.

The selections in this book are intended to convey the history of architecture as developed in Illinois. Partiality has been shown for diverse geographical and chronological representation as well as a variety of buildings. Historical significance has sometimes been a heavy factor in the selection, but always where the monument itself was architecturally appealing as well. Attention has been paid to architects whose contribution is identified with the growth of the state. Architecture has always been a single expression of a many-sided condition; the social pattern of life, the aesthetic and emotional response to environment, the economic and technological factors—all varying with the decades —have made their impact on Illinois architecture. A summary can only sketch the major aspects of its history.

The French settlement of Illinois country did not begin until 1699, with the Cahokia mission, and it expired with the Treaty of Paris in 1763 which gave England control of land east of the Mississippi. This period of French building was characterized by the palisade type of construction not so very different from Norman farmhouse building. The technique remained peculiar to the French river settlements and did not resemble English half-timbering, which had been adapted in the eastern colonies. French ideas continued into the early nineteenth century and became a part of a vernacular river style of southern Illinois. The Pierre Menard house (1802) near Chester and the Rose Hotel (1814) at Elizabethtown are examples.

The shift from river to prairie settlements began in the early nineteenth century with pioneers arriving in search of good farms, a search which led over-land, often following Indian trails. They built crude log cabins, first as homes and then as churches, schools, and even public buildings. Immigration into the state increased greatly after the Black Hawk War of 1832 which ended the Indian menace.

The architectural growth of the state in the 1830's and 1840's was considerable and dramatic. The expedient pioneer log structures were replaced by an ambitious vernacular architecture. Its style was initially a post-Colonial manner absorbed from knowledge of eastern buildings. Carpenters, masons, and bridge builders trained in the older states did most of the competent work. There was little need for the profession of architect, though John F. Rague, one of Illinois' earliest, is known to have established an architectural practice in Springfield about 1831. It was he who won the commission for the first capitol in Springfield. When elaborate designs were desired, architects from outside the state were sometimes consulted. St. Louis, for example, had several architects in the 1820's and was known as a source of sophisticated design in the Midwest.

One of the most significant American building techniques, second only to the skyscraper, was the balloon frame which first appeared in Chicago in the early 1830's. Balloon framing is a simplified, light wood construction using machine-sawed lumber and machine-made nails. It replaced the eastern brace frame which consisted of laboriously shaped, heavy timbers fitted together with elaborate joints and wooden pegs. The very lightness of the new frame gave rise to the derisive term "balloon," which became its name. The frontier city of Chicago was a logical place for the development of this quick and easy technique of building, an innovation which was partly responsible for the rapid rise of St. Paul and San Francisco as well.

This first phase of architectural maturity was based not only on an assimilation of late Colonial traditions but also on enthusiasm for the rising Greek Revival. Ohio and Michigan, then Indiana and Illinois, fell before its advancing popularity. In Illinois the Greek Revival was sometimes manifest in ambitious works such as the Old Shawneetown Bank (1836), but more often it was found in the wood frame houses of farm and village in which classical details were freely adapted to the ability of the carpenter and shaped to the nature of the material. One cannot overlook the many classical courthouses, temples of justice for the new counties, which exemplified the civilizing influence of architecture. The beautiful and skilled work of the Greek Revival is the most satisfying aspect of the early architecture of the state.

Romanticism in architecture had another side, the Gothic Revival, which appeared in distant Illinois almost as early as in the eastern states. Jubilee College (1839) and St. Peter's Church at Grand Detour (1848) are examples. The fashion for Gothic arose from the cult of the picturesque and was first introduced as an alternative style appropriate to certain buildings. Eventually the Gothic and more generalized medieval variations challenged the fitness of the Greek Revival to express the variety of architectural demands. Also questioned was the moral propriety of the pagan classic to shape the architecture of a Christian nation. Classical precedents, particularly the temple form, came to be regarded as stifling. Experimentation with other styles followed, and by the mid-century the state of architecture was one of rampant eclecticism. Alexander Jackson Davis, a versatile designer himself, listed the choices available to a home-owner: "American Log Cabin, Frame House, English Cottage, Collegiate, Gothic Manor House, French Suburban, Switz [sic] Cottage, Lombard Italian, Tuscan from Pliny's villa at Ostia, Ancient

Etruscan, Suburban Greek, Oriental, Moorish and Castellated."

This mid-century freedom of choice opened the way for the hybrid styling of the post-Civil War period. Loosely known as the Victorian style, it has sometimes been scorned as "bourgeois baroque." Yet the visual rewards of Victorian design are again being won by those disenchanted with the puritan simplicity of modern architecture. Once disdained for their ostentation and complexity, such nineteenth-century examples are now recognized as architectural events full of entertainment and satisfaction, in addition to having been functional solutions of their time. The Victorian house articulated the idea of special rooms to suit special purposes. The development of vacation hotels with their promenades of wooden porches anticipated the casualness and association with nature that were the goals of early modern architecture.

Reaction to the pompous elaboration of post-Civil War architecture is seen in the work of Henry Hobson Richardson. Although his early work partook of Victorianism, he soon changed to the Romanesque style and modified it to become his personal signature. From his studio in Brookline, Massachusetts, his influence rapidly spread. Richardson's picturesque side is seen in Altgeld Hall on the University of Illinois campus in Champaign-Urbana. His simplified manner, for example the serene arcading of his Marshall Field warehouse in Chicago (1886, destroyed 1931), influenced Louis Sullivan and the architects of early Chicago skyscrapers. While Richardson himself was on the threshold of modern architecture, Sullivan brought these beginnings to maturity, and later Frank Lloyd Wright shaped the same ideas into more dynamic form.

By 1890, soon after his death, Richardson's Romanesque style had lost much of its popularity. A more hardened, academic approach was coming in. Even the work of his successor firm, Shepley, Rutan and Coolidge, was Renaissance inspired, as seen in their Art Institute (1892) and Public Library (1895) in Chicago. The most dramatic display of this new Classic-Renaissance manner was the enormously successful 1893 World's Columbian Exposition held in Chicago, the site of which is now Jackson Park. In addition to putting a definite end to Richardsonian Romanesque, the Exposition declared Chicago to be the leading city in the Midwest.

Beginning in the 1880's, the commercial expansion of Chicago created a great demand for office buildings in the Loop. The expediency of this building activity developed the first true skyscraper building in the world. It was William LeBaron Jenney's Home Insurance Building of 1883–85 (destroyed 1931) that first assembled the ingredients of skyscraper construction: a metal frame, properly fireproofed, with an elevator for vertical trans- portation. Although not a very handsome building, its technological significance was unmistakable, and the technique, soon copied in New York, was known thereafter as "Chicago construction."

The technical problems of the skyscraper were comparatively simple whereas the aesthetic ones were not. It was Louis Sullivan who, as champion of the architect's creativity, gave us his version of the skyscraper as a tall and soaring element. His designs were original and never historical, and were always marked with his peculiar genius for ornamentation. Other architects, equally bold—such as the firm of Holabird and Roche—saw the skyscraper as a more rational and disciplined form. Their designs expressed more directly the nature of the metal skeletal frame.

Besides Sullivan's particular contribution to the aesthetic expression of the skyscraper, he was the recognized spiritual leader of modern American architecture. His influence on his pupil, Frank Lloyd Wright, and others, resulted in a progressive Midwest group unequalled anywhere in the country. Wright eventually surpassed his master and became America's best-known architect. His designs were as dynamic and provocative as his personality. His first mature phase, from 1900 to 1910, produced probably his best work. Unfortunately for architecture, the earnestness and ability of this midwest group, George Elmslie and George Maher among others, had dissipated by about 1920.

The progressives lost their lead with the return to historical eclecticism, an architecture of taste, understanding, and skill, rooted in European traditions. In architecture the work of Howard Shaw, Charles Platt, and David Adler best represents tnis phase; in planning it was Daniel Burnham's plan for Chicago, inspired by the baroque cities of Europe. Much of this reactionary spirit in design can be traced to the success of the 1893 Exposition.

Yet this interest in civic art made its real contribution in setting a bold and comprehensive pattern for urban design. Chicago led the nation in the "city beautiful" movement. Part of Burnham's scheme was the planning of ring highways and parkways. His concern for green spaces resulted in new parks and the Forest Preserve District of Chicago and Cook County. In this effort Jens Jensen, a local landscape architect of international reputation, must be mentioned for his sensitivity to the beauties of the prairie landscape.

In the 1930's, echoes of the modern movement in Germany and Holland were heard; and later in that decade such eminent design leaders as Mies van der Rohe and Moholy-Nagy emigrated to this country and settled in Chicago to teach and practice. Their arrival meant a continuation of the new European ideas, especially the *Bauhaus* principles which had been established by Walter Gropius at his famous school in Dessau. Thus architecture regained its modern orientation and, while little was done during World War II, postwar building saw the decided influence of these European ideas. Chicago in particular has seen a revival of commercial building in recent years that rivals the great building activity of the 1880's. Outstanding in this recent work is the Inland Steel Building (1957), the first new office building in the Loop in many years. It is a dramatic example in stainless steel and glass of contemporary skyscraper design. Such buildings have made the public at large more aware and more appreciative of the nature and purpose of modern architecture. The practice of historical eclecticism seems forever dead.

Curiously enough, with the acceptance of a modern style, a growing public has become increasingly aware of our nation's architectural heritage. Historical societies and preservation groups are actively at work to save the best of the past and to prevent the needless disappearance of this heritage. It is now fortunately recognized that historical buildings of diverse styles and meanings give breadth, perspective, and meaning to our civilization. It is this very sympathy and understanding that have made this book possible.

I wish to thank the many persons who have given their help, among whom are Harold Allen, Paul M. Angle, Carl W. Condit, Caroline R. Heath, G. William Horrell, Margaret A. Flint, George M. Irwin, Marguerite S. Kaufman, James C. Massey, Robert Rodriguez, Ruth E. Schoneman, Carlisle F. Smith, Mrs. Evelyn Snyder, Armour Titus, and Philip A. Turner. I also wish to thank Mrs. Helen Geraghty and the staff of the Illinois Sesquicentennial Commission for their constant assistance.

Frederick Koeper

Note: Selections recorded by the Historical American Buildings Survey have been marked *HABS*.

Photographic Credits

Harold Allen: 17, 43, 139, 151 *top,* 157 *bottom,* 159, 169 *top* and *bottom,* 193, 209, 217, 281. Wayne Andrews: 5, 111, 161, 163, 245, 279. Bahá'i Headquarters: 295. *Belleville News-Democrat:* 7, 9. Ray M. Brown: 167. Orlando R. Cabanban: 107. Chicago Aerial Photo: 89. *Chicago's American:* 91 *right.* Chicago Architectural Photo Company: 69, 75. Chicago Association of Commerce & Industry: 77 *top.* Curtis & May: 31 *bottom.* Deere & Company: 149. Robert Deschler: 261. Frank Fenner: 301. Herbert George Studio: 179. HABS: 11, 49, 51 *bottom,* 55, 99, 113, 123, 125 *left* and *right,* 133 *bottom,* 141, 177, 181, 203, 211 *top* and *bottom,* 227, 249. *Hedrich-Blessing:* 45, 53 *bottom,* 59, 61, 65 *top* and *bottom,* 73, 77 *bottom,* 79, 81, 83, 87, 91 *left,* 93 *top* and *bottom,* 127, 131, 133 *top,* 145 *top* and *bottom,* 165, 185, 191, 195, 199, 219, 229, 255 *bottom,* 265, 285, 287, 289, 291, 293 *bottom,* 297. Winfred Helm: 269. G. William Horrell: 3, 23, 25, 27, 29, 31 *top,* 39 *top* and *bottom,* 109, 147, 157 *top,* 175, 223, 225, 267. Otis Hutson: 183. Illinois College: 155. Illinois Information Services: 15, 129, 137, 207, 215 *top.* Illinois State Historical Society: 271, 273. International Harvester: 153. Helmut Jacoby: 97. Leslie H. Kenyon: 275 *top* and *bottom.* Baltazar Korab: 89. Clarence Laughlin: 47 *top.* Brooke Lemburg: 213 *top* and *bottom.* Edgar Lundeen: 19, 101. Mildred Mead, Chicago Historical Society: 135. *National Geographic:* 215 *bottom.* Nauvoo Restoration, Inc.: 197. Ron Neilsen: 53 *top.* Richard Nickel: 51 *top,* 57, 67. Quincy Society of Fine Arts: 193 *bottom,* 231 *top* and *bottom,* 233 *top* and *bottom,* 235, 237, 239. Ricker Library, University of Illinois: 21, 189, 283; Olivia Scully: 103; Ezra Stoller (ESTO) for Deere & Co.: 187 *top* and *bottom. St. Louis Post-Dispatch,* Scott Dine: 105. Armour H. Titus: 251, 253, 257 *top* and *bottom,* 259 *top* and *bottom.* Phillip Turner: 47 *bottom,* 63, 71, 85, 115, 117, 119, 121 *top* and *bottom,* 143 *top* and *bottom,* 171, 173, 205 *top* and *bottom,* 241, 243, 293 *top.* Union Tank Car Company: 299. University of Illinois, Chicago Circle: 95. University of Illinois, Urbana: 35. United States Army: 255. Washington University: 221 *top* and *bottom.* Webster Brothers: 13.

Illinois Architecture

Stinson Memorial Library, *Anna*. 1914.

2   This library and community center was designed by Walter Burley Griffin, an associate of Frank Lloyd Wright in the Oak Park studio from 1902 to 1906. During these years Griffin (1876–1937) assisted in such works as the Larkin Building in Buffalo (1904) and Unity Temple in Oak Park (1906). Wright's architecture of this period had an obvious effect in shaping Griffin's style as an independent architect.

Stinson Memorial Library, designed in 1912 and built two years later, is a small building but of monumental scale. The pair of massive entrance pylons, here stucco over brick, and the high position of banded iridescent windows recall Wright's designs. More personal is Griffin's choice of local fieldstone for the powerful texture of the walls. He used the sloping site to advantage, providing the required auditorium at a lower level, with large windows at the rear and a separate side entrance.

Griffin was a graduate in architecture of the University of Illinois. His interest in landscaping and city planning culminated in his 1912 award for a master plan for the capital city of Canberra, Australia, where he ended his career. He had the able assistance of his architect-wife, Marion Mahony (1873–1962), who also shared his experience in Wright's Oak Park studio.

Address: 409 South Main Street.

Old Second National Bank, *Aurora*. 1923

4   The parody of banks, libraries, and churches masquerading
     as Greek and Roman temples was opposed by Louis
     Sullivan and his followers. George Grant Elmslie (1871–
     1953), who had worked for many years for Sullivan,
     designed this bank building in the creative spirit of his
     master. It is one of the three buildings he did in Aurora.
     Its base is constructed of pink granite from New Hampshire
     and its walls of a golden-brown brick, long and narrow in
     proportion and laid with raked mortar joints. The exterior
     is monumental and dignified without being unduly formal.
     The sculptured blocks that surmount the piers flanking
     the entrance symbolize civic and agrarian growth. These
     were done by Emil Zettler. The banking-room interior
     continues the warm colors of the exterior and contains a
     large mural of early Aurora (1835) by John W. Norton.

     The planned facilities for this bank building are unusual.
     Besides banking areas, the building contains a public
     auditorium with a seating capacity of two hundred in the
     front part of the basement. Offices occupy the third floor.
     The fourth and fifth floors provide social and dining
     rooms for a private club. In the brochure printed for the
     building's inauguration, the owners proclaimed, "What
     our Architect has done on the Building is to give us a
     genuine interpretation of our needs on sane, rational
     and economical lines, and it is illustrative of what a
     native Architectural product may be."

Address: 37 South River Street.

St. Clair County Courthouse, *Belleville*. 1857–61 and 1893.

6   In 1785 Thomas Jefferson and an assisting French architect, C. L. Clérisseau, prepared a design for the Virginia state capitol based on a Roman temple in Nîmes, France. This design for Richmond was the beginning of neoclassicism in architecture. Functional offices were put inside a temple envelope. This approach became a durable formula for state capitols and county courthouses which was used with variations throughout many decades.

The St. Clair County Courthouse is a splendid example of this long tradition. It is unusually tall in proportion and is constructed of limestone and red brick. The project, the third county courthouse in Belleville, began in 1850 with a design prepared by a Richard Barrett. Actual construction did not begin until 1857 when members of the court acted as contractors under the direction of an architect named Robert Mitchell. It is uncertain if the courthouse design follows Barrett's original scheme or a new one prepared by Mitchell. The 1857 building measured sixty by ninety feet. An extensive rear portion was added in 1893, doubling the length of the building and adding side wings and a dome as well. This extension was done by architects Bailey and Kroener of Henderson, Kentucky.

Address: Public Square.

Dobschutz House, *Belleville.* 1866.

8   This example of domestic architecture combines the
     compact and symmetrical plan of earlier Georgian and
     neoclassic houses with the decorative interest of the
     Victorian age. A center hall and a corner kitchen are
     included within its rectangular plan. The house is
     constructed of red brick and ornamented with lintels and
     railings of cast iron. Decorative ironwork was a by-product
     of the industry of Belleville, a city renowned as the stove
     capital of the Midwest. (The chimneys of this house were
     obviously made for stoves and not for fireplaces.) A
     modest bracketed cornice supports the eaves of the
     metal-covered roof.

     The property was originally part of a militia grant made to
     Major Nicholas Jarrot after the Revolutionary War. The
     Dobschutz House and its terraced garden are being
     restored as the museum of the St. Clair County
     Historical Society.

Address: 701 East Washington Street.

Hildrup House, *Belvidere.* 1855.

10   The plan of the Jessie S. Hildrup House is a forty-foot
      square including the two-story Doric portico across
      the front. A one-story kitchen ell extends to the rear. A
      center stairhall divides pairs of rooms on either side, a plan
      similar to the earlier James Dowling House in Galena.
      The Hildrup House uses a side entrance and a pyramidal
      roof and is simpler and bolder than the Galena building.
      The approach to the house originally was set with an
      allée of trees on axis with the front door. The house is now
      part of the Plantation Motel. *HABS.*

Address: North State Street.

Oasis Restaurant, *Belvidere*. 1957.

12   The development of elaborate automobile highway systems has resulted in the corollary architectural problem of designing service stations and restaurants along the routes. On the Northwest Tollway, Interstate 90, at Belvidere and elsewhere, restaurants have been designed as bridgelike structures which span the highway and can be used by patrons traveling in either direction. Not only is this a striking solution to a modern problem, but by consolidating facilities in one building, savings in building and operating costs were made. The architects were Pace Associates.

Road view of Oasis Restaurant
Air view of a cloverleaf highway intersection

Old Colony Church, *Bishop Hill*. 1848.

14   Bishop Hill, a Christian communist colony, was settled in 1846 by a group of Swedish immigrants headed by Eric Janson. The first winter many of the colonists lived in caves. After this uninviting beginning the colony developed rapidly, and in a few years the colonists were tilling more than twelve thousand acres of fertile prairie land. With handmade tools and simple machinery various industries were started.

The first permanent building erected in Bishop Hill was this church, which served as an apartment building as well. It is framed in heavy oak timbers pegged together. The church proper is on the second floor under the gambrel roof. On the first floor and in the basement is a total of twenty living rooms divided by a wide center corridor. Crude bricks of mud and straw were used in the partitions, and the exterior is a simple sheathing of clapboards without pretension. The architectural effort of these Jansonists is seen inside their church, which is fitted with carefully made altar, communion rail, and pews. The present chandeliers are copied from an original found in the balcony. The church is owned by Bishop Hill State Park. *HABS*.

Address: Bishop Hill Street and Maiden Lane.

Steeple Building, *Bishop Hill*. 1853.

16   The architecture of the Jansonist colony soon developed
      into a competent classical style and was of such quality as
      to indicate that architectural values were part of the
      colony's idealism. We do not know who designed the
      buildings that surround the public square. Some of them
      are of brick with an overcoating of stucco.

      The most striking of the Jansonist efforts is their Steeple
      Building, which is a sophisticated and almost Renaissance
      design. It was built as a hotel, but never used as such,
      because the railroad came through nearby Galva,
      diminishing the importance of the carriage road through
      Bishop Hill. Instead, the building was used as a colony
      apartment house. The construction is of brick with a
      plaster surface. The stucco plaster is worked into a
      rustication pattern for the first story and into pilaster strips
      and window framing above. Originally the roof had a
      wood balustrade. The cupola design is particularly
      beautiful and contains a functioning handmade clock.
      The Steeple Building is owned by the Bishop Hill Heritage
      Association. *HABS*.

Address: Main and Bishop Hill Streets.

The David Davis Mansion, *Bloomington*. 1870–72.

18   Judge David Davis was a close associate of Abraham
      Lincoln in law and politics. In 1862 Lincoln appointed him
      to the Supreme Court, from which he resigned in 1877
      to become senator from Illinois. In 1883, at the end of his
      term, Davis returned to Bloomington to live in this
      house which he had built earlier.

      The compositional features of the design relate to the
      popular books published by Andrew Jackson Downing
      Cottage Residences of 1842 and *Landscape Architecture*
      of 1844. Primarily a gardener, Downing favored a suburban
      landscape setting for various informal house styles and
      was opposed to the rigidity of the Greek Revival. Among
      his book illustrations was the Italian villa or Tuscan style
      whose composition was marked by a campanile tower and
      bracketed eaves. He also favored porches and bay
      windows. The Davis house is a development of this
      mid-century trend and suggests similar designs built in
      the East by Henry Austin and Alexander Jackson Davis. The
      architect of the Davis house was Alfred H. Piquenard.

      Robust and substantial, like Judge Davis himself, the house
      is built of yellow brick from Milwaukee and trimmed
      with limestone quoins and window frames. The
      pedimented porch, the Palladian window above, and the
      mansarded tower show a heartier architectural appetite
      than the more restrained examples set forth by Downing.

      The Davis Mansion is now administered by the Illinois
      State Historical Library as a museum of nineteenth-century
      life. *HABS*.

      Address: Monroe and Davis Streets.

Cahokia Courthouse, *Cahokia. ca.* 1737.

20   The first permanent white settlement in Illinois country
     was founded in 1699 at Cahokia by Father Jean François
     Buisson de St. Cosmé. Here too is the earliest surviving
     building in the Midwest, the Cahokia Courthouse.
     Originally built as a home, it was bought in 1763 by a
     French military engineer, Captain Jean Baptiste Saucier,
     whose son François sold it in 1793 for use as a county
     courthouse and jail. Cahokia was then the seat of a
     judicial district of St. Clair County, Northwest Territory.

     The building is a modification of the earliest French
     construction, *poteaux-en-terre,* upright logs set in trenches
     with the spaces between filled with *bouzillage,* a mixture
     of clay and grass. The wood used in Illinois was usually
     cedar. Later a timber sill was added to support the wall
     (poteaux-sur-sole), as seen in this example. The origin of
     this palisade log construction is uncertain, though some
     versions resemble French Norman building.

     The courthouse was dismantled and moved to St. Louis
     for the 1904 Exposition. It was then moved to Chicago
     where a fourth of the original building was set up in
     Jackson Park. In 1939 it was returned to Cahokia. In its
     reconstruction, stone infilling has been substituted, and
     shingles have replaced what was probably a thatched
     roof. *HABS.*

Holy Family Church, *Cahokia. ca.* 1790.

22   The mission of the Holy Family established by Father St.
      Cosmé in 1699 originally had a wood church, but this fell
      into decay after the departure of Father Forget about
      1763. The mission was revitalized in 1787 with the decision
      to build a new church using the ruins of Father Forget's
      house: doors, windows, and their frames, as well as
      some boards. In construction it followed the French
      palisade method and resembled similar churches being
      erected in the St. Louis area at the same time. None remain
      but this church, probably the oldest church still standing
      in the Mississippi Valley.

      The wall construction is of massive vertical hewn timbers,
      seven inches thick and ten to twelve inches wide, spaced
      about nine inches apart and braced diagonally at the
      corners. The edges of these posts were channeled to
      receive a filling of lime and rubble *(pierrotage)*. Walls,
      not vertical, slope inward some five inches from bottom
      to top on all sides—another feature typical of the Illinois
      French carpentry. Originally, ceiling boards covered the
      heavy trusses within which were not meant for display.

      It is uncertain when the church was completed, but the
      finished building was noted in 1797. In September, 1799,
      it was solemnly blessed and named the Church of the
      Good Shepard. It is now known by its original name.

      In 1833 two side wings were added, one for a sacristy and
      one for an organ and choir. The church was restored
      in 1950. *HABS.*

Jarrot House, *Cahokia*. 1799–1806.

24   Adjacent to the Holy Family Church in Cahokia stands the
        Jarrot House, the oldest brick structure in Illinois. It was
        built by Major Nicholas Jarrot for his second wife, Julie
        St. Gemme de Beauvais. Major Jarrot, a refugee from the
        French Revolution, made a fortune in fur trade and land
        speculation and was once a judge of the Cahokia court.
        He was also known as a lively host of dancing and
        gambling parties which were held in the ballroom on the
        second floor of his house.

        The Jarrot House is well constructed of brick with
        eighteen-inch-thick exterior walls. Black header bricks are
        used in every sixth row to achieve a horizontal banding
        effect. Interior partition walls are also of brick. In
        architectural design the Jarrot House is late Colonial
        rather than in the Creole tradition. It is a companion piece
        to the William Henry Harrison House in Vincennes,
        Indiana.

        The house was occupied by the Jarrot family for eighty
        years. Afterwards it was used as a school and convent
        building. It is now planned to restore the house as a
        historic building of St. Clair County. *HABS.*

Halliday-Rendleman House, *Cairo*. 1865.

The southermost town in Illinois is Cairo, standing at the
junction of the Ohio and Mississippi rivers. Its strategic
location made it a busy port in the steamboat era, and
subsequently it became a railroad center as well. The city
was a link between the North and the South and was
made a strong Union outpost at the beginning of the
Civil War.

At the end of the war, Captain William Parker Halliday
anticipated the coming prosperity and lavishness of Cairo
in building this handsome white-painted brick house
which is now named "Riverlore." The mansard roof is
covered with slate set in geometric patterns and is crested
with an ornamental iron railing. Although he was then
president of Cairo's first bank, Captain Halliday's earlier
steamboat career prompted him to build a "captain's walk"
atop the third story, from which he could view the river
traffic. The architect of the house is unknown.

Although the house does not contain many rooms, they
are spacious and well detailed. An oval, cantilevered
stairway winds its way up to the lookout some forty feet
above. On the third floor is a small private theater
complete with workable stage. The interior details reflect
the ornate French styling which was beginning to
influence American taste. Its decorative colored-glass
windows and rich plasterwork are exceptional.

In 1900 the house was bought by Dr. John J. Rendleman
who lived there until his death in 1952.

Address: 2723 Washington Avenue.

Custom House and Post Office, *Cairo*. 1869–72.

28   In 1826 a German architect, Heinrich Hübsch, wrote a
pamphlet entitled "In Which Style Should We Build?" He
advocated a combination of styles and argued that new
and beautiful forms were impossible. His answer
summarizes the nineteenth century's position of
architectural eclecticism.

In addition to the major revivals, Greek and Gothic, other
styles entered the competition for popularity. In the
Custom House and Post Office in Cairo, for example, we
see Romanesque and Renaissance features combined. The
details of the first floor and the over-all symmetry of the
building are Renaissance. The couplet windows and the
severity of the upper floors suggest Romanesque. It is a
sedate and serious design executed by A. B. Mullett
(1834–90) who was appointed supervising architect
of the Treasury in 1865. The main floor was given over
to the post office; the second floor provided offices for
government officials; and the third floor was devoted
to the U.S. district court. The courtroom was splendidly
executed and furnished, with arched ceiling, columned
walls, three-tiered chandelier contributing to the grand
effect. When it was opened, the *Cairo Daily Bulletin*
noted: "The room is said to be the neatest courtroom in
the United States, such being the deliberately expressed
opinion of Architect Mullett on his last visit of inspection
to the custom house, when he surveyed with much
satisfaction the entire building."

With the completion of a new post office in 1942, the
building was deeded to the city of Cairo. It is now used as
Police Headquarters.

Address: Washington Avenue and Fifteenth Street.

Magnolia Manor, *Cairo*. 1869–72.

30   The flour milling merchant, Charles A. Galigher, who
      built this house has left us with an ornate example of the
      Italianate Victorian style. His house is of local fired red
      brick and stone with substantial wood trim and
      ornamental cast-iron verandas. The brick masonry of the
      window and door openings above the ground floor is
      rimmed with a grooved and rounded brick which forms
      a recessed, beaded frame. Within these openings are wood
      window frames designed with a twisted rope pattern.
      The console window heads are of fabricated sheet metal.
      The exterior cornice and eaves brackets are of wood
      millwork.

      In 1952 the house was acquired by the Cairo Historical
      Association and renamed Magnolia Manor. It is main-
      tained as a public museum with many of its original
      furnishings intact. These interiors—with wooden classical
      columns, a walnut spiral balustrade, decorative plaster
      cornices, Carrara marble fireplaces, ornate chandeliers,
      and heavily carved furniture—are especially fine. The
      decorative taste of the 1870's is complete before us:
      an overnourished splendor of high Victorian design
      reflecting a self-assurance and vigor unchastened by
      scholarship. The true creativity of the Victorian period is
      only beginning to be acknowledged.

Address: 2700 Washington Avenue.

Entrance to Magnolia Manor
Parlor interior

32   The history of the building of this courthouse is a notorious one, centering on its excessive cost, which plunged the county into debt for forty-three years. Originally a sum of $50,000 was voted, but the completed work ran to $1,380,000. The courthouse came into existence only after long litigation and heated opposition. The four commissioners in charge, assisted by Governor John M. Palmer, himself a Macoupin County resident, ultimately triumphed over the anti-courthouse party who tried to stop the work and challenged the legality of the ever-increasing bond issues. Funds were undoubtedly mismanaged, for the building cost exactly twice its worth. Over the years a courthouse bond tax reduced the debt. In 1910 the last remaining bond was ceremonially burned in the courthouse square while every bell and whistle in every city, town, and hamlet in Macoupin County sounded for five minutes.

Architecturally the courthouse is a magnificent structure solidly built of brick, limestone, and iron, and virtually fireproof throughout. Stairs and doors are of iron. The basement level is vaulted stone. The top floor, largely occupied by the courtroom, is 32 feet in height. The iron dome rises 186 feet above its foundation. Corinthian porticoes terminate the north and south facades. Its solid columns are constructed of huge segments of stone. Originally, gilded lampposts and a surrounding iron fence and iron gateways embellished the composition. Even the sidewalks were once of limestone. Understandably, it was without architectural equal in the entire Midwest.

The architect of the building was E. E. Meyers of Springfield, also the architect of the Jersey County Courthouse in Jerseyville.

Illini Assembly Hall, *Champaign*. 1961–63.

34 Two bowl-like forms enclose a vast columnless and windowless arena whose purpose can be adapted to various sporting events or theater uses. The roof portion is constructed as a folded plate shell of reinforced concrete. The lower portion is set 24 feet below grade and is cradled by 48 radial buttresses. Its interior slopes are arranged to seat 16,400 persons. The glazed two-story perimeter lobby serves admirably without concealing the structural shapes.

The covering dome spans 400 feet. Its folded pattern is revealed both on the exterior and within. The folds extend to a maximum depth of seven and one-half feet. Located at its outer edge is a post-tensioned ring consisting of six hundred miles of quarter-inch wire. The directness with which the functional and engineering aspects have been expressed, and the happy absence of architectural embellishment, have created a heroic and satisfying image.

The architects were Harrison and Abramovitz; the partner in charge was Max Abramovitz (1908–   ), a graduate in architecture of the University of Illinois. The structural engineers were Ammann and Whitney.

Canal Lock House No. 6, Illinois and Michigan Canal, near *Channahon. ca.* 1845.

The Illinois and Michigan Canal, greatest of the canal systems in the Midwest, was a triumph of early enterprise and contributed immeasurably to the growth of Chicago and northern Illinois.

Louis Joliet, who accompanied Marquette over this low divide, first suggested the building of the waterway in 1674. In 1820 a first survey was made, and two years later Congress granted a right-of-way and authorized construction. The first earth was turned in 1836, but owing to the scarcity of funds and to many legal and technical complications, it was not until 1848 that the first boats passed through. By 1862 there were more than seven thousand canal boat clearances annually and in one year more than a million tons of freight. With the development of railroads, and the opening of the parallel and much larger Chicago Sanitary and Ship Canal in 1900, decline was inevitable, and the last freight barge was locked through about 1905.

Lock No. 6 and Lock No. 7, and accompanying spillways, feeder, and dam, constitute an outstanding example of pioneer engineering as it successfully solved the problem of carrying the canal across the DuPage River. The lock house was built in Lockport, seat of canal operation, and transported to the site. *HABS.*

Address: Near U.S. Route 6.

Pierre Menard House near *Chester*. 1802.

38 In 1703 a Jesuit mission was established in a village of Kaskaskias, a tribe of Illinois Indians. Kaskaskia thus became the second white settlement in what is now Illinois. Together with Cahokia and Fort de Chartres, Kaskaskia was a center of French life in the American Bottom, linked by river transportation with New Orleans. Kaskaskia was the territorial capital and then the first state capital between 1809 and 1820. It had begun to decline even before it was washed away when the Mississippi River changed its course in 1881.

The sole surviving example of French architecture in this vicinity is the Pierre Menard House, situated at the base of the bluff opposite the village site. Menard was a Quebec-born fur trader and a government official of the Illinois Territory and state. His house is typical of French colonial style, having low and broad proportions, one main story, dormer windows, and a spacious porch. The house is now a state memorial.

Address: Fort Kaskaskia State Park.

Extended front porch of Menard House
Interior of the detached kitchen

Little Mary's River Covered Bridge, *Chester.* 1854.

Among the historic landmarks of Illinois are its nine remaining covered bridges, several of which are still in service. Probably the oldest covered bridge in Illinois is this one which spans eighty-eight feet across Little Mary's River. It has a clearance of seventeen feet across and eleven feet high. It was constructed as part of a seven mile toll road from Chester to Bremen, built by the Randolph County Plank Road Company. Both bridge and road were owned and operated by a Mr. Hartmann until 1872 when they were purchased by the county. The bridge continued in public use until 1930. In 1936 the bridge and the adjacent property were donated to the State of Illinois as a historic park site.

All of the timber in this bridge is original, with the exception of the floor, floor joists, roof, and siding. Its construction is a combination of truss and strengthening arch, a system devised by the famous pioneer bridge builder, Theodore Burr (1762–1822). The Burr system and the Town Lattice Truss were equally popular in Illinois. The timbers of the bridge are of handhewn, native white oak with different members joined together with tree nails or "trunnels." When the bridge was restored in 1955, some steel reinforcement was introduced. Among the wood replacements was a new roof of cedar shake shingles which replaced the hickory ones. Roofs and sidings on such bridges were necessary to protect the supporting timber framework from weathering.

Address: Five miles northeast of Chester on Ill. 150.

Clarke House, *Chicago*. 1836.

42   This house was one of the two most elaborate houses in
     Chicago of its time, the other being the William B. Ogden
     House, also erected in 1836. The Ogden House was
     destroyed by the fire of 1871, but the Clarke House
     remains as the oldest in Chicago. Originally it stood near
     16th Street and Michigan Avenue. Its first owner, Henry
     B. Clarke, died in 1849, and it was occupied by his widow
     until 1872 when it was sold and then moved to its present
     location by the new owner. At that time its front portico
     and roof balustrade were removed and a cupola built. The
     house is remarkable for its lofty main-floor rooms. *HABS*.

Address: 4526 South Wabash Avenue.

Water Tower, *Chicago.* 1867–69.

On tree-lined Michigan Avenue stands Chicago's most cherished monument of the nineteenth century—that toy castle, the Water Tower. It was completed before the great fire of 1871 and survived that disaster which destroyed much of the adjacent pumping station. Both structures were restored in 1910–13. The fanciful castellated Gothic style of the Water Tower is more reminiscent of the eighteenth-century *Gothick* follies than of the Victorian period. The rough-faced yellow limestone, once much used in Chicago buildings, was quarried near Joliet. The Water Tower's architect was William W. Boyington (1818–98), whose Rose Hill Cemetery Gates (1893) are of similar design.

The purpose of this tower was to encase a three-foot-in-diameter wrought-iron standpipe 138 feet high, providing a hydrostatic head to equalize the pulsation of the pump and thereby assuring a continuous flow. Drinking water was drawn from Lake Michigan two miles out through giant wooden pipes to the pumping station. Modern equipment has made this standpipe feature obsolete.

Boyington was born in Southwick, Massachusetts, and after some architectural study in New York, he had a peripatetic career as architect before coming to Chicago in 1853. His practice as designer and contractor was substantial both before and after the fire. He was the architect of hotels and commercial buildings as well as of seven Chicago churches. His most imposing building was perhaps the old Board of Trade of 1882–83 (destroyed 1929) done in the high Victorian style. *HABS.*

Address: Chicago and Michigan Avenues.

Wood Mansion, *Chicago.* 1882.

46   Not all Victorian design in this country was inspired by European precedent. The truly American flavor and character of this period can be seen in the Wood Mansion. The placing of mantel and fireplace, the recessed buffet, and the brass chandeliers are among its original features.

The original owner, George Ellery Wood, was a lumber millionaire. The house is now owned by Charles Boyd and has been carefully restored even though it was in ruinous condition when purchased in 1948.

Address: 2801 South Prairie Avenue.

Interior of the dining room
Exterior of Wood Mansion

Glessner House, *Chicago*. 1886.

The John J. Glessner House is one of the last works of
Henry Hobson Richardson (1838–86) and the only one
remaining of four he built in Chicago. The fortress-like
granite exterior yields to a more domestically scaled
courtyard within. Richardson was one of the most sought-
after architects of his day. After schooling at Harvard
University and the Ecole des Beaux Arts in Paris, he soon
established a preference for the Romanesque style, using
heavy masonry and picturesque features such as towers
and gables and round arches. His 1872 Trinity Church in
Boston is the key example of his early period.

Richardson's subsequent designs made it clear, however,
that he was to rule over the style and not the style over
him. The result was an increasing simplicity and grandeur
in his work. This coherence and direction in the midst of
the architectural confusion of the post-Civil War period
was keenly felt among his contemporaries. Wrote Ralph
Adams Cram, "In this maelstrom of horrid revelations and
hesitant hopes, Richardson burst upon an astonished
world as a sort of saviour on high. . . ."

Richardson's ability to compose freely in plan and elevation mark an independence radical in his time. The proto-
modern statement made by Richardson was developed by
Sullivan and further expanded by Wright, the three
forming a triumvirate of progressive American architects.

The Glessner House is now used by the Chicago School
of Architecture Foundation. *HABS*.

Address: 1800 South Prairie Avenue.

Rookery Building, *Chicago*. 1886.

The Rookery is a transitional building, part of which was built in a masonry wall-bearing construction and part in a skeletal frame. The architects, Burnham and Root, fared well with both techniques.

The principal elevations facing LaSalle and Adams Streets are constructed of brick and granite masonry with a diversity of treatment: columns, piers, and arches; smooth and rough masonry; lively ornament juxtaposed to powerfully plain surfaces. The decoration and articulation of these elevations testify to the lingering picturesqueness in commercial architecture as well as the persistence of the masonry wall.

The other exterior elevations, and those that form the interior light court, are of quite different construction: here an iron frame supports the masonry. Notably in the light court one can see the regularity that is forced into the design by this construction—a forecast of the consistent rhythms found in modern office buildings. The openness gained by this construction is also obvious.

The ground-floor lobby is covered with a glass and iron skylight (now painted over) and embellished with fanciful iron stairways. It was sympathetically remodeled by Frank Lloyd Wright in 1905. *HABS.*

Address: 209 South LaSalle Street.

Interior of lobby court
Detail of west elevation

Auditorium Building, *Chicago*. 1887–89.

52   One of Chicago's most celebrated landmarks, the
      Auditorium Building is the joint effort of two architects,
      Dankmar Adler (1844–1900) and Louis Sullivan (1856–
      1924). To combine a hotel, office building, and auditorium
      in a single structure is a difficult architectural problem,
      and the challenge provided these architects with oppor-
      tunities for their respective talents: Adler's grasp of
      engineering matters and acoustics, Sullivan's gift for
      architectural composition and ornament. With this
      building Sullivan reached his full maturity, absorbing
      Richardson's grandeur and developing his own brilliance
      in decoration. Adler designed the intricate interior iron
      framing and shaped an acoustic masterpiece in the theater.
      Both contributed to the tower portion which forecast the
      skyscraper tower form of the Schiller-Garrick Theater
      and other buildings.

      The Auditorium Building became Roosevelt University in
      1946. The reopening of the beautifully restored theatre in
      the fall of 1967 marked the end of a successful campaign
      to return to Chicago its most memorable interior. *HABS*.

Address: Michigan Avenue and Congress Street.

Gilded plaster ornamentation of Auditorium Theatre
Exterior view

Grand Central Station, *Chicago.* 1889–90.

54 The railroad station of the nineteenth century was a wholly new architectural problem without historical precedent. Basically its requirements were twofold: there must be a waiting room and offices, and a train shed for arriving and departing trains. In Grand Central Station, the architect, Solon S. Beman (1853–1914), has given us a severely handsome brick exterior with a commanding clock tower 222 feet high. The L-shaped brick portion partially encloses the vast train shed composed of wrought-iron semicircular trusses springing from the platform surface. In appearance and function Grand Central Station is one of the most distinguished railroad stations in the country. It is presently owned by the Baltimore and Ohio Railroad. *HABS.*

Address: South Wells and West Harrison Streets.

Manhattan Building, *Chicago*. 1889–91.

56   The productive years of Chicago building 1880–1900
produced the pioneer skyscrapers of the world. Of several
architects connected with this momentous period, William
LeBaron Jenney (1832–1907) stands out as the one man
who designed the first acknowledged skyscraper, the
Home Insurance Building (1883–85) which was
destroyed in 1931.

The Manhattan Building is a representative example of
Jenney's subsequent work. Originally it was twelve stories
high flanked by nine-storied wings. Its front and rear
façades illustrate a diverse treatment of window openings,
and even more variety was seen when Jenney added four
more floors to the central block. Some of the projecting
bays are trapezoidal, some triangular. Elsewhere large
sheets of glass fit simply into the structural framework.
Near the top of the final building an arcaded motif was
introduced. This mixture was to prove uncharacteristic
of later skyscraper designs.

It was in the engineering aspects of skyscraper development that Jenney made his greater impact. In his Manhattan
Building he introduced both diagonal and portal types of
wind bracing. Another innovation was the cantilevering
of the floors along each property line to avoid overloading
the footings of the adjacent buildings. Thus the weight of
these outermost bays is carried by the second file of piers.
The exploratory achievements of Jenney are truly historic
for the rise of the skyscraper in America. *HABS*.

Address: 431 South Dearborn Street.

Newberry Library, *Chicago*. 1890–93.

58   Henry Ives Cobb (1859–1931) was a notable Chicago
      architect whose Richardsonian Romanesque predilections
      were no doubt shaped by his education at M.I.T. and
      Harvard, close to the Brookline fountainhead. As a busy
      young architect in Chicago he was chosen in 1888 by the
      trustees of the newly established Newberry Library to
      design the library building. Cobb was unfortunate in
      having to please a strong-willed, architecturally minded
      librarian, Dr. W. F. Poole. Poole had a national reputation
      for his anti-monumental, anti-book-stack theories in
      library design, and his opinions prevailed over Cobb's
      in the final plan.

      The resulting library building is a restrained, Renaissance-
      like composition whose façade breaks into five orderly
      units reflecting the compartmented arrangement within.
      The exterior details of Spanish Romanesque which Cobb
      adapted are not employed for plastic or picturesque effects
      as in Richardson's own work; the façade is most orderly
      and somewhat severe.

      The Newberry Library was esablished in 1887 by the
      bequest of Walter Loomis Newberry, a pioneer Chicago
      merchant. It is a privately maintained research library
      open to scholars. *HABS.*

Address: 60 West Walton Street.

Monadnock Block, *Chicago*. 1891.

60   More than a half-century ago Montgomery Schuyler
      pronounced the Monadnock Block the best of all office
      buildings. Even today it is a favorite among architects.
      Curiously, its construction was not at all up-to-date: it is
      a brick masonry bearing wall sixteen stories high built at a
      time when complete steel skeletons were becoming
      standard practice. Yet evidence tells us that it was intended
      to be done entirely in steel, and the change was apparently
      the wish of the Boston client, Peter Brooks.

The architect, John Wellborn Root (1851–91) of the firm
Burnham and Root first struggled with the Monadnock
design early in 1884. Brooks made it quite clear that he
wanted a simple building. "My notion," he wrote to his
Chicago agent, "is to have no projecting surfaces or
indentations, but to have everything flush. . . . So tall and
narrow a building must have some ornamentation in so
conspicuous a situation . . . [but] projections mean dirt,
nor do they add strength to the building . . . one great
nuisance is the logment of pigeons and sparrows. . . ."

In reporting Root's progress with the design, the agent
wrote to Brooks, "His head is now deep in Egyptian-like
effects, and he declares that if he fails to make a
harmonious and massive and artistic building this time,
he will never build another office building." Root's
finished work was eminently successful. Ironically his
early death never gave him the opportunity to design
other office buildings. The tapering slab with its subtle
refinements which is the Monadnock stands as a
monument to Root's great ability. *HABS*.

Address: 53 West Jackson Boulevard.

62 This museum was originally the Palace of Fine Arts for the World's Columbian Exposition of 1893. The great success of the fair was largely due to its imposing classical architecture. The layout focused on a Court of Honor, a formal lagoon set with a golden Statue of the Republic by Daniel Chester French. White classical buildings of uniform scale lined each side of the lagoon and were spectacularly lighted at night. Five eastern and five Chicago architects cooperated in a united effort guided by Daniel H. Burnham (1846–1912). The noted landscape architect, Frederick Law Olmsted (1822–1903) was in charge of the site plan. "As a scenic display, Paris has never approached it," said Henry Adams. "The greatest meeting of artists since the 15th century," wrote Augustus Saint-Gaudens. Only a minority thought the architecture was too eclectic, too European in its inspiration.

The Palace of Fine Arts was designed by Charles B. Atwood (1848–95), in the office of D. H. Burnham and Co. It was rebuilt between 1929 and 1940 and is now the Museum of Science and Industry in Jackson Park.

Address: 57th Street and South Lake Shore Drive.

Carson Pirie Scott Store, *Chicago*. 1899, 1903–4.

64 In 1895 Louis Sullivan began to practice alone after the break with his partner, Dankmar Adler. Although this was in some respects a less successful phase of his career, it nonetheless included the important Schlesinger and Mayer commission of 1899. The store became Carson Pirie Scott & Co. in 1904.

In this design Sullivan has afforded us those dual pleasures of architecture: an involvement with decoration as well as the satisfaction of discipline and order. The exuberant cast-iron ornament of the lower two floors—much of which was done by Sullivan's loyal assistant, George Grant Elmslie—is perhaps the most persuasive statement for the use of decoration in architecture. The upper floors, set with crisp and tranquil horizontal windows, are a terminal statement of the Chicago window theme. The total building, however, is less than perfect due to the stages in which it was built and to the uncomfortable, curved corner portion (probably a demand of the client) which ill suits the spirit of the design.

Louis Sullivan was regarded then and is regarded now as the spiritual father of modern American architecture. His writings and buildings forcefully assert the position of the architect as a creative individual and the need for an architecture related to society. *HABS.*

Address: 1 South State Street.

Exterior view
Ornamental detail of corner entrance

Carl Schurz High School, *Chicago*. 1908–10.

66 Dwight H. Perkins (1867–1941) was an architect of the Chicago School who trained at M.I.T. and in the office of Burnham and Root. In 1893 Perkins set up his own office, and later, between 1905 and 1910, he was associated with the Chicago Board of Education. During these years he produced many designs which set a high standard for school buildings.

Perkins' best school is probably the Carl Schurz High School, a majestic composition dominated by vertical piers in brick and a steeply pitched roof of red tile. A central block is flanked by diagonally placed wings, and the whole is well placed on the open site. *HABS*.

Address: Milwaukee Avenue and Addison Street.

Robie House, *Chicago*. 1909.

68   Robie House and "Falling Water," the Kaufmann house in
      Pennsylvania, are Frank Lloyd Wright's most admired
      houses. Although thirty years apart, both illustrate Wright's
      preoccupation with the balcony theme, first timidly
      expressed in his Charnley House design of 1891 in Chicago,
      done in the office of Adler and Sullivan, and last in the
      Guggenheim Museum in New York, where a continuous,
      spiraling interior balcony comprises the entire scheme.

      Here in the Robie House, Wright has manipulated three
      levels—starting with a sunken terrace "balcony" below
      the pavement which serves the billiard room and play-
      rooms. The piling up of horizontals, not the least of which
      are the shooting cantilevered roofs at either end (cunningly
      supported by hidden steel channel beams), is held in
      equilibrium by the vertical piers and pylons and by the
      chimney, which acts as a masonry spindle for the whole.
      Compressed, intense, and inward-looking, it is a design
      that overwhelms its narrow site, a miniature of a
      multi-walled medieval city.

      The Robie House stands together with the Coonley House
      in Riverside as a terminal statement of Wright's prairie-
      house period. Although then without much American
      recognition, these early Wright designs were published in
      Germany in 1910 and 1911 and did much to support
      progressive architecture abroad.

      The Robie House now serves as the Adlai Stevenson
      Institute of International Affairs of the University of
      Chicago. *HABS.*

Address: 5757 South Woodlawn Avenue.

Church of St. Thomas the Apostle, *Chicago*. 1922.

70   Barry Byrne (1883–1967) was a member of that group of
      Prairie School architects who got their start in Frank
      Lloyd Wright's Oak Park studio just after the turn of the
      century. Byrne's importance as an architect is not to be
      measured by the similarities of his work to Wright's,
      however, but by the differences. Early in his career he
      abandoned Wright's more flamboyant forms and simplified
      his buildings. With warmth of color and humanness
      of scale, Byrne achieved a modern functionalism without
      loss of feeling which has earned him a distinctive place in
      the history of architecture.

      The Church of St. Thomas the Apostle marks the beginning
      of his illustrious career in designing modern churches.
      The wide airy space of the light-filled nave which flows
      easily into the sanctuary startled churchmen accustomed
      to the removed and shadowed recess common to most
      sanctuaries. Byrne united the two spaces, nave and
      sanctuary, thus anticipating the reforms that were not to
      come about in Catholic liturgy for forty years. In the
      intervening decades Byrne designed churches for nearly a
      dozen major midwestern cities. In these, all traces of
      medieval fustiness are removed. His churches unite
      modern technology with modern taste and modern
      man's spiritual needs.

Address: 5472 South Kimbark Street.

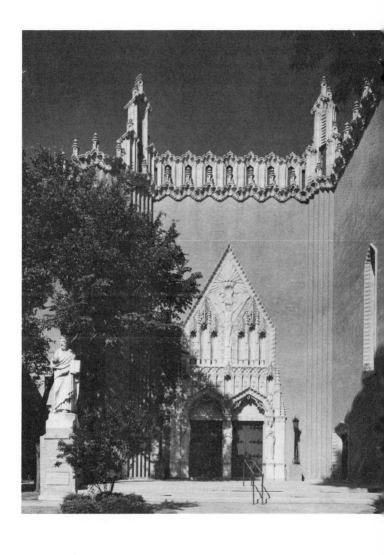

Tribune Tower, *Chicago*. 1922–25.

72   The arrival of the skyscraper caught the architect unprepared. He was unsure of how to design a suitable exterior for a tall steel skeleton. "The triumph of commerce and the despair of art," lamented architect John Head Howells in 1902. The earlier Chicago sky-scrapers appeared to be nothing but enlarged warehouses, and seemed to ignore the aesthetic way pointed by Sullivan. However irrational it may seem today, the architect turned to historical ornament as a design solution, with varying degrees of success. The Gothic style was particularly favored because its inherent verticality was thought expressive of the tall building scheme.

In 1922 the *Chicago Tribune* announced an international competition for a new headquarters building. The first prize was won by Howells (1868–1959) and Raymond Hood (1881–1934) for their design based on the early sixteenth-century "Tour de Beurre" of Rouen Cathedral and the tower of Malines. Thus French and Belgian Gothic served as one solution to a twentieth-century problem. The executed building suggests a masonry-bearing building stiffened with steel rather than a steel frame building sheathed in stone. In this respect it represents the nullification of the Chicago tradition. Nevertheless, its handsome lantern makes a graceful transition to the sky and provides sculptural relief to the blunt outlines of newer buildings on Chicago's skyline.

Address: 435 North Michigan Avenue.

Rockefeller Memorial Chapel, *Chicago*. 1925–28.

74 Bertram G. Goodhue (1869–1924) was one of the
outstanding Gothic Revival architects in America. He
trained for six years under James Renwick, famous as the
architect of St. Patrick's Cathedral, and between 1891
and 1914 was a partner of Ralph Adams Cram. In 1918 the
University of Chicago asked him to prepare a design for
a chapel for which John D. Rockefeller stipulated
$1,500,000, a fraction of his total gift to that institution of
$34,700,000. Goodhue's original suggestion was for a
fortress church reminiscent of Albi, but he shifted to a
Gothic design in keeping with the existing buildings by
Henry Ives Cobb, the first planner and architect of
the university.

Goodhue's design consisted of five generous vaulted bays
with an impressive tower serving as the east transept. The
interior groined vaulting is of Guastavino glazed tile
whose color relieves the cold and somber limestone
interior. The interior and exterior sculptures were the work
of Lee Lawrie and Ulric Ellerhusen.

Goodhue died before the building was begun. He is
commemorated as the figure of Architecture on the south
side of the tower door holding in his hand a model of
his chapel.

Address: 59th Street and Woodlawn Avenue.

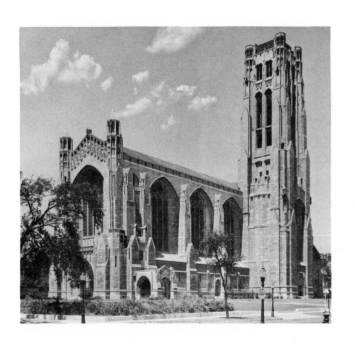

Buckingham Fountain, *Chicago*. 1927.

In 1909 Daniel H. Burnham (1846–1912), with the aid of
Edward H. Bennett (1874–1954), presented a comprehensive plan for the city of Chicago. A major aspect
of this proposal was the development of part of the
lakefront which became Grant Park. The actual filling in
had begun in 1904 and the park was completed in the
1920's. From Randolph Street to Twelfth Street a
grand-scale design was planned east of Michigan Avenue,
befitting the city whose tall buildings now form a
backdrop to Burnham and Bennett's lakefront design.

On axis with Congress Street is Buckingham Fountain.
Said to be the world's largest fountain, it is modeled after
a similar one at Versailles and was designed by Jacques
Lambert. It is fitted with 133 jets of water, with the
height of the main column reaching 135 feet.

Address: Grant Park at Congress Street.

Buckingham Fountain
Air view of Grant Park and Chicago skyline

Lady Esther Plant, *Chicago*. 1937.

78   When modern architecture came to a focus in Europe in the 1920's, one of its aims was to express visually the function and construction of contemporary buildings. Although its hostility to historical designs and ornamentation was understandable, the results were sleek and mechanical designs, often unrelieved by modeling or variations in composition. Yet the effect could be fresh and satisfying after a surfeit of overornamentation.

Perhaps this early modern period, often called the "International Style," found its ideal expression in the factory building. Such an example is the Lady Esther Plant by Albert Kahn (1869–1942). Its regular rhythms and over-all simplicity make it an excellent illustration of this initial phase of contemporary design.

Although self-educated in architecture, Albert Kahn was an outstanding architect of industrial and commercial buildings. His designs combined beauty with utility. His innovations include the under-one-roof factory planning and—later and more revolutionary—the one-floor straight-line production which is illustrated in this plant. In architectural detail, the fenestration recalls early designs of Walter Gropius and Erich Mendelsohn in the 1920's.

Address: 7171 West 65th Street at South Harlem Avenue.

860–880 Lake Shore Apartments, *Chicago*. 1951.

It is a happy accident of architectural history that the career of Ludwig Mies van der Rohe (1886–   ) in Chicago renewed the tradition of rational steel-framed construction which was initiated in the city in the 1880's.

Preparatory to the multi-story designs Mies van der Rohe executed in this country were his various paper projects done thirty years earlier in Germany. This long gestation bore results in the most celebrated of his tall buildings, 860–880 Lake Shore Apartments. The structural rhythm of uniform bays and uniform floors is dramatically and clearly expressed. Equally straightforward are the finlike mullions (steel I-beams painted black) and the aluminum window frame. A gratuitous I-beam mullion is welded to each structural support to sustain the regular rhythm set by the others.

The theoretical directness of these identical twin towers has been much admired and much debated. For Mies van der Rohe there is no controversy, only the continuous search for expression in architecture of the two major forces at work in society today, economics and technology. Only in accordance with these factors can one achieve an architecture truly expressive of our epoch.

Address: 860–880 Lake Shore Drive.

Crown Hall, Illinois Institute of Technology, *Chicago.*
1956.

From 1938 to 1958 Ludwig Mies van der Rohe served as
chairman of the architecture department of the Illinois
Institute of Technology. In 1940 he devised a master plan
for a new campus for the school comprising a number
of low, steel-framed buildings whose studied arrangement
was guided by a twenty-four-foot modular grid. Buildings
and separating areas were to be considered a
unified whole.

Only part of this campus scheme was built. Of those
buildings designed by him, Crown Hall, serving the
department of architecture, is the most impressive. It
reveals two major influences in Mies van der Rohe's work:
the formality of classicism and the structural rationalism
of Viollet-le-Duc. In materials and methods it reflects
the twentieth century: huge welded plate girders and vast
sheets of glass. Its main floor is but a single space 120
feet by 220 feet, formed by a floating roof suspended from
the underside of four girders which in turn are supported
by eight steel columns. The single room is without
permanent or structural subdivisions and is intended to
lend itself to changing groupings or architectural
classes within.

The simplicity of Mies van der Rohe's architecture is
deceptive. Diverting and arbitrary forms are nowhere
seen; instead the eye is drawn to the meticulous detail,
proportion and placement of the essential parts. The rigor
of this architectural approach suggests to some an
aesthetic purity, to others a chilling finality.

Address: South State and 34th Streets.

Laird Bell Law Quadrangle, University of Chicago, Chicago. 1960.

84   This group of four linked buildings is dominated by a six-story library whose cantilevered floors are enclosed by a boldly beveled, glass curtain wall. Administrative offices, classrooms, and auditorium are arranged to form an entrance court dominated by a large reflecting pool. The architects were Eero Saarinen (1910–61) & Associates. The sculpture in the pool is by Antoine Pevsner, the Russian sculptor.

The problems of the site included a nearby neo-Gothic dormitory which Saarinen recognized in continuing in his own design its small, broken scale, irregular silhouette, and verticality. The design is without recourse to the specific details of the Gothic style, however; the building is sympathetic yet wholly modern.

Not shown is the two-story structure containing auditorium and practice courtroom. Its faceted stone exterior continues the themes of the library, and its isolated sculptural form recalls the polygonal chapter houses of English monasteries.

Address: 1111 East 60th Street.

Marina City, *Chicago.* 1961–63.

86 The twin cylindrical apartment towers of Marina City are to Chicago what the Eiffel Tower is to Paris: the architectural identification of the city. Graceful and imaginative balcony forms begin above eighteen stories of a helix parking ramp, assuring tenants an advantageous view of the crowded city below. The confined urban site of only 3.1 acres is relieved by the adjacent river which has justified the inclusion of boat-docking facilities. Also assembled on the site are a sixteen-story office building and a separate television auditorium studio. Within the complex are various facilities such as a restaurant, a bank, shops, a bowling alley, and a skating rink. Marina City is a dramatic solution to the architecturally difficult problem of urbanism. It combines residential and commercial uses; it offers individuality and convenience; it succeeds in imparting that sense of excitement, pleasure, and choice that only a large city can provide.

Not the least of Marina City's achievements is its structural design. Reinforced concrete construction is used with Fiberglas lined molds to achieve smooth surfaces. Each tower rests on six-foot thick concrete slabs which in turn rest on forty concrete caissons reaching a depth of over one hundred feet. The central core of each tower contains elevators, stairs, and ducts. Around these cores are arranged the radial plans of 896 apartments. The architects and engineers were Bertrand Goldberg Associates; the consulting structural engineer was Fred Severud.

Address: 300 North State Street.

O'Hare International Airport, *Chicago.* 1963.

88   The scale of twentieth-century building is becoming increasingly larger and more difficult to reconcile with the scale of the individual. In the design of a major airport, for example, highways and parking areas on one side, and vast runways on the other, present a difficult yet unavoidable setting for the terminal building itself.

At O'Hare International Airport the architects, Naess and Murphy, have maintained an appropriately large scale, have provided spacious interiors, and have relieved congestion with a double-deck approach roadway.

Civic Center, *Chicago*. 1964–66.

The presence of Mies van der Rohe and his work in Chicago has provided that city with architectural inspiration and a yardstick for achievement. It is appropriate, therefore, that the design of the recently completed Civic Center should pay tribute to this eminent architect. The rigorous clarity of its framing and the symmetry of its design recall the lessons of the master. The architect-designer directly responsible for this building is Jacques Brownson, who was once a student of Mies van der Rohe.

The Civic Center is essentially a steel-frame office building, but one which has heroic and symbolic presence in the midst of Chicago's Loop. It is distinguished from its commercial neighbors by its monumentality, derived from studied simplicity and large scale. The amplitude of its eighty-seven-foot bays is truly impressive. The oxidizing steel used for the exterior is a bold choice for a civic building. The granite-paved plaza which covers the entire block forms an appropriate setting for this magnificent structure. At its base stands Pablo Picasso's gift to the city, a steel-plate sculpture whose benign image surveys the active city scene.

The architects for the Civic Center were C. F. Murphy Associates with Skidmore, Owings & Merrill and Loebl, Schlossman & Bennett Associates.

Address: Randolph and Dearborn Streets.

View of the Civic Center
Chicago's Picasso sculpture

U.S. Courthouse and Federal Office Building,
Chicago. 1964–66.

92   This building is the first of three which will comprise a new
federal center for Chicago. A second office building and
a post office are to be built on a square city block opposite
the completed building. This grouping is designed as two
high-rise blocks and a low post-office building. The
disciplined architectural detailing is characteristic of
Ludwig Mies van der Rohe who designed the complex.
A. E. Epstein and Sons and C. F. Murphy Associates were
the associated architects of this project.

Address: Dearborn and Jackson Streets.

Reflections in glass of Federal Courts Building
Model showing finished grouping

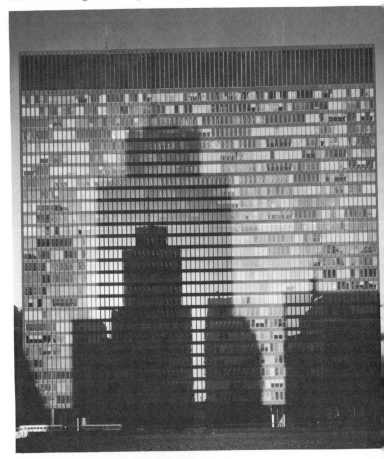

University of Illinois, Chicago Circle, *Chicago*. 1965.

94   The new Chicago Circle campus of the University of
      Illinois is a striking example of planned growth of
      facilities for higher education. Preliminary designs were
      begun in October, 1958, and the first phase of construction
      was completed for occupancy by 7,000 students in
      February, 1965. A Chicago branch of the University of
      Illinois had existed at Navy Pier since 1946.

      The site of 106 acres is immediately southwest of Chicago
      Circle freeway interchange and adjacent to subway
      connections, a wise choice for a commuting student body.
      The master plan separates buildings by function rather
      than by departmental organization for economy and
      flexibility. Visually the campus is composed of a juxta-
      position of small elements in the center with large
      buildings at the outer edge in order to reconcile the
      heroic scale of adjacent freeways with pedestrian campus
      life. Much use is made of bold textures and geometric
      forms to give individuality to the buildings. Architecturally
      it expresses that departure which began in the mid-1950's
      away from the more sober and rationalistic designs of the
      early modern period.

      The supervision architects were Skidmore, Owings &
      Merrill, who were responsible for the majority of buildings.
      The architects for the Student Union Building were
      C. F. Murphy & Associates.

Address: Halsted and Harrison Streets.

John Hancock Center, *Chicago.* 1966–68.

96 The Chicago tradition of multi-purpose buildings established by Adler and Sullivan's Auditorium Building is continued in the hundred-story Hancock Center which combines 29 floors of offices with 48 floors of apartments and 23 other floors devoted to shops, parking, and other amenities. Its tapering form was in part suggested by the lesser floor area required for apartments above than for office floors below and in part by engineering considerations.

This steel-framed skyscraper of 1,107 feet is the tallest building in Chicago and the second tallest building in the world. A prominent aspect of the exterior is the visually expressed diagonal wind bracing, a feature which was modest and concealed in the early skyscrapers of the 1890's. Before being applied to buildings, such bracing had long been used in bridge construction. Its first American use other than in bridges may have been Gustave Eiffel's interior framework for the Statue of Liberty (1883–86). Here in the Hancock Center the bracing assumes a dominant role, apart from structure, in delineating segments and thereby conveying a sense of scale and measurement to the towering shaft.

The exterior is of black anodized aluminum and tinted glare-absorbing glass. The architects and engineers of the Hancock Center were Skidmore, Owings & Merrill.

Address: 875 North Michigan Avenue.

Grosse House, *Columbia*. ca. 1858.

98   This attractive house is an example of early building by
the German settlers of Columbia. It was built by John
Grundlach for A. Grosse who operated a tavern and had an
interest in a brewery down the street. Grosse stored surplus
beer in a stone vault under his own house.

Of red brick, once painted, the house displays an
architectural ambition common to the homes of successful
townsfolk in Columbia. The center doorway is treated as
a recessed classical portico and the window lintels are
of decorative cast iron. The house has changed little in
appearance; only a rear porch has been added. *HABS.*

Address: 625 North Main Street.

Millikin House, *Decatur*. 1876.

The assertive individualism of the post-Civil War period is best displayed in the rich man's house. The James Millikin mansion in Decatur is an example. Its ancestry is in the tentative eclecticism of Alexander Jackson Davis and Richard Upjohn, whose "Bracketed" or "Tuscan" villas of the 1840's established a basic freedom in house design as opposed to the Greek Revival style. Such designs were amenable to additions and variations for many decades, and even classical elements found their way back into part-time usage—as seen in the pediments of the Millikin House. Its tall narrow proportions and tower with mansard roof are characteristic of the 1870's. When built, it was the finest mansion in Decatur.

Whether an elaborate Victorian house is a proper work of architecture is an argument heard less often as passing years lend respectability and interest to the Victorian age. Once regarded as an unstable and ostentatious phase of American fashion, late nineteenth-century work is being critically re-examined. Aesthetic fatigue with sleek and undecorated modern architecture has also aided its popularity.

James Millikin was a banker and founder of James Millikin University (1901). His house became the Decatur Art Institute in 1917 and the Decatur Art Center in 1944, at which time it also became officially connected with Millikin University.

Address: 124 North Pine Street.

Pioneer Gothic Church, *Dwight.* 1857.

The history of Dwight began in 1853 when James C.
Spencer and an associate drove through this countryside
surveying the railroad from Chicago to St. Louis. It must
have been Mr. Spencer who decided the train would
stop at Dwight, because he subsequently bought land and
became the town's founding father. That year a pole
with a tin can on top was all there was of Dwight; a year
later there were two small shanties and a water tank for the
railroad engines. It is an indication of the speed with
which the West was developed that by 1857 Spencer was
contributing part of the $2,620 to build a Presbyterian
church, the first church in the village.

The unknown architect-builder created an example of
American carpenter Gothic which has survived more than
a century. The church is entirely of wood frame with
random width boards and triangular battens. Door and
windows are accented with vigorous mouldings. For almost
a decade the church doubled as a school, and much of
the political and social life of Dwight must have taken
place within its walls. It was used in turn by a Danish
Methodist (1892), a Christian Scientist (1924), and a
Baptist congregation. This excellent example of vernacular
American Gothic is now owned by the Dwight Historical
Society which is restoring it as a general meeting hall
for the village.

Address: North Franklin and Seminole Streets.

Eads Bridge, Mississippi River, *East St. Louis.*
1868–74.

Early proposals (beginning in 1839) for spanning the
Mississippi River at St. Louis were for a wire cable
suspension bridge. In 1867 James B. Eads (1820–87)
proposed to span the river with three enormous tubular
arches, each span being more than five hundred feet,
set between two masonry piers and two abutments sunk
to bed rock. Eads was without experience as a bridge
builder, but his knowledge of the river bed and currents,
gained through salvage of sunken steamers, gave him and
his backers confidence in his design.

The construction of the piers was a more difficult aspect
of the bridge building. During a trip to Europe, Eads
consulted with English and French engineers about their
well-advanced pneumatic caisson technique, and upon
his return in April, 1869, he employed it for the first time in
the United States. Work was started that summer on
the Illinois pier, which presented the more formidable
problem due to the greater depth of bed rock that would
be encountered. Work on the piers was completed only
after the loss of numerous lives.

The construction of the arches was relatively easy and
safe. These were erected by cantilevering the tubular
segments with the aid of backstays to the abutments and
piers. Eads substituted steel for the conventional cast
iron and was the first to do so, thus also anticipating the
first architectural use of steel by fifteen years. The upper
deck carries a roadway, the lower a double-track railway.
The Eads Bridge stands as a durable and handsome
example of American engineering.

University Center, Southern Illinois University, *Edwardsville*. 1966.

Southern Illinois University, chartered by the state in 1869, established its first permanent buildings at Carbondale. Recently, a new campus was established outside Edwardsville, and classes began in September, 1965.

The first phase of construction on this campus consisted of six major buildings designed by Hellmuth, Obata & Kassabaum who were responsible, together with Sasaki, Dawson & De May Associates, for site planning as well. Instead of submitting to the pastoral setting, the architects have created a vigorous and assertive image in scale with the open countryside. All six buildings are of red brick and precast concrete with an aggregate surface. The massing of the University Center building, like the other five, is boldly cubistic. The strong color and texture contrasts continue into the interiors which are correspondingly bold and dramatic.

The master plan of the twenty-seven-thousand-acre Edwardsville campus shows a complex of more than twenty academic and service buildings together with the projected development of recreation areas and land for biological and scientific research. Housing facilities and professional schools may become part of future plans.

Address: Ill. 157 southwest of Edwardsville

Rose Hotel, *Elizabethtown*. 1814.

Elizabethtown, situated on a bluff overlooking the Ohio
River, was once an important steamboat stop for trade and
passengers. The town was founded by James McFarland
and named for his wife. The west section of the hostelry
originally called McFarland's Tavern was built by him
in 1814. Major additions were made to the building in
subsequent years, including a sample room for traveling
salesmen to display their merchandise to buyers from
the surrounding countryside. The hotel was owned by the
McFarland family for three generations.

In 1891 the hotel was purchased by Mrs. Sarah E. Rose who
operated it from 1884 until her death in 1939 at the age of
eighty-seven. Since that time her daughter, Mrs. Rose
Gullett, has been its owner. It is the oldest continuously
operated hotel in Illinois. The pleasant two-story porch is a
survival of the vernacular French architecture of the
Midwest.

Buck Hall, Principia College, *Elsah*. 1931–37.

110   The design of a new college campus involves more than
       bricks and mortar; it becomes an environment which
       molds the ideals and character of its students. For this task
       Principia College chose Bernard Maybeck (1862–1957), a
       famous California architect whose personal style later
       inspired the informal Bay Region architecture of post-
       World War II. His Bingham House in Montecito (1917)
       was designed for the father-in-law of Principia's director,
       a commission that led to this one.

       From the start, both the architect and Principia College
       agreed that an English village, with its informally placed
       buildings set among the trees, should serve as a model. For
       the design of various units Maybeck borrowed from the
       medieval, but not without making it his own. Coupled
       with his artisan's sense of traditional materials and
       textures was his curiosity about new methods of
       construction—sprayed concrete, for example. He
       experimented with various effects and materials on the
       tiny "Mistake House," as it is known, now a Maybeck
       museum. While Maybeck's master plan was never
       completely realized, a sufficient number of buildings were
       built to his design to convey the idealism and picturesque
       vision of the architect.

Willard House, *Evanston.* 1865.

112   Frances E. Willard was an active teacher, temperance
      crusader, and advocate of women's rights. She served as
      first dean of women at Northwestern University and was
      one of the organizers of the international Woman's
      Christian Temperance Union.

      Headquarters for Frances Willard's activities was her
      parent's home, which she called "Rest Cottage." It is an
      informal frame house set with steep gables trimmed
      with decorative bargeboards. These Gothic suggestions
      are reinforced by vertical board and batten siding. The
      porches and bay windows were standard features in
      American domestic architecture throughout the second
      half of the nineteenth century. Willard House was
      designated a national historic site in 1965. *HABS.*

      Address: 1728 Chicago Avenue.

Grossepoint Lighthouse, *Evanston*. 1873.

114   The navigation of Lake Michigan by early ship captains was
       extremely hazardous; there were no aids to navigation
       the whole length of the lake, and the Chicago harbor was
       without obvious natural identification. In 1831 the
       federal government built the first lighthouse for the
       Chicago area near the mouth of the Chicago river, but it
       collapsed before it could function. The following year
       its more durable successor sent out a feeble beam from
       a fourteen-inch reflector.

       By 1870, traffic in the port of Chicago numbered more
       than twelve thousand ships annually. However, rotting
       piers and dangerous sandbars formed navigation hazards
       about the port, and a government report recommended
       transferral of the lighthouse to Grosse Point, thirteen miles
       away.

       The construction of the Evanston lighthouse, the oldest
       lighthouse structure in Illinois, is of brick which was given
       a concrete covering in 1914 to repair the effect of erosion.
       The lantern was fitted with a Fresnel lens made in France.
       Its inventor, Augustin Jean Fresnel, developed the first
       practical and efficient apparatus using refraction of light
       rays rather than reflection, which was the former method.
       The Grossepoint lens is still in use, though the kerosene
       oil lamp was replaced by an electric one in 1935. The
       lighthouse has been deeded to the city of Evanston
       and the keeper's house has become a nature museum.

Address: 2535 Sheridan Road.

Dawes House, *Evanston.* 1894.

116   The bastion towers of the château of Chambord may have suggested the front elevation of this French-inspired mansion built by a New York architect named F. Edwards Ficken. The walls are of yellow brick and the roof of red tile. Although the grounds are beautifully landscaped, the exterior of the house is of less interest than the interiors, which form a succession of richly styled rooms executed without restraint. Attention to craftsman-like details which were once a part of architecture is everywhere apparent: for example in the specially made lighting fixtures by Louis Tiffany.

The house of twenty-eight rooms was built for the Rev. Robert D. Sheppard of Northwestern University and was acquired by Charles Gates Dawes in 1909. Dawes served as vice-president from 1925 to 1929. He lived in this house until his death in 1951. It was willed to Northwestern University with the wish that it be occupied by the Evanston Historical Society, and it is now their permanent headquarters. Dawes's keen interest in the history of the Northwest Territory and his book collection make this an appropriate historical center.

Address: 225 Greenwood Street at Sheridan Road.

First Congregational Church, *Evanston*. 1927.

118   The architect of this church was Thomas Tallmadge
       (1876–1940), a prominent architect of the Chicago area and
       an architectural historian. He had a special knowledge
       of, and affection for, English Georgian architecture and its
       American colonial equivalent.

       Tallmadge's predilection is revealed in this Georgian-styled
       design which recalls the suave churches of James Gibbs
       of early eighteenth-century London. It is built of red
       brick with limestone trim. The portico, belfry, and spire
       are also of stone. The interior is later in inspiration,
       suggesting Robert Adam.

       The church is the third Congregational Church building on
       the site. The congregation was organized in 1868.

Address: Hinman Avenue and Lake Street.

Lindheimer Astronomical Research Center at
Northwestern University, *Evanston*. 1967.

120   The current expansion of the Northwestern University
        campus is on a seventy-five acre site created by filling
        in part of Lake Michigan. The second structure to be built
        on this site is the observatory for two telescopes housed
        in separate domed observation rooms, 24 feet and 36
        feet in diameter. The individual telescopes are anchored
        separately to the ground, and the rooms themselves are
        supported by a welded tetrahedron structure partially clad
        in corrugated steel. The design of this support was chosen
        because it provided the least exposed surface, minimizing
        expansion and contraction caused by changes in night
        and day temperatures. The architects were Skidmore,
        Owings & Merrill.

Distant view
Double facilities of the observatory

Keating House, *Fayville. ca.* 1841.

The Keating House is a solitary reminder of various attempts to settle the west bank of the Fox River north of St. Charles. An early settler was Rice Fay who arrived in 1834. Eventually a few stone houses together with a small store and a blacksmith shop became known as Fayville. Two years later, in 1836, a Baptist minister named David W. Elmore bought nearby land from a squatter and expanded his holdings to 400 acres. He laid out some of his land near the river in generous lots with streets 100 feet wide. He named his ambitious town Asylum. The area was also known at various times as Five Islands, Riverside, and Silver Glen; but today all five names are without a village.

The Keating House was purchased by John Keating from its builder, Rice Fay, shortly after it was completed. It is constructed of rubble stone walls with dressed stone lintels, sills, and quoins. The two chimneys on each end are of brick and stone. It is not known whether the kitchen ell is original or a later addition. *HABS*.

Address: North of St. Charles on Route 31 at MacLean Boulevard.

Nicholas Dowling Store, *Galena. ca.* 1840.

124   This example of commercial building is typical of the
       straightforward, simple design seen in the first half of the
       nineteenth century. Later the use of cast-iron store fronts
       resulted in more elaborate designs. The entrance to
       the Dowling Store is framed by limestone piers and lintels
       with recessed wood framing and glass. Above are three
       floors of Galena-made brick set with well-proportioned
       windows. A distinctive element of the façade was a
       cast-iron balcony whose balustrade spelled out the name
       of the store. It was made by Nicholas Dowling himself
       who operated a foundry at the rear of the building. *HABS*.

Address: Diagonal Street.

Drawing of original elevation
Present view of Dowling Store

Hoge House, *Galena*. 1845.

126   In its westward sweep, the last wash of the Greek Revival
       was deposited on the banks of the Mississippi. The
       "templed hills" of Samuel Francis Smith's 1832 hymn
       remind us of the ubiquity of that style in the American
       landscape, a style later referred to by its detractors as the
       "Greek mania."

       An example of the temple portico architecture which was
       adapted to all manner of buildings is the Joseph Hoge
       house built for a Baltimore lawyer who came to Galena
       about 1838. The architect-builder, Henry I. Stouffer, was
       from St. Louis. The four-column Doric temple design is
       complete, with its broad base of steps and extended
       entablature, but such classical considerations are limited
       to the façade, and, indeed, are somewhat overpowering
       for the scale of this modest brick house. Frontispiece
       architecture is admittedly a thin involvement with style,
       but it does evoke, as in this example, associational values
       of a bygone age. *HABS.*

       Address: 512 Park Avenue.

Old Market House, *Galena*. 1845–46.

128   Local limestone, brick, and wood are used in the
construction of this public building, which served as a
market until 1910. Upstairs was a council chamber, in use
until 1936. In 1947 the Market House was deeded to
the state and restored to its original condition. It has four
columnar porches of modest architectural detail. On
its roof is a square cupola, each face of which is decorated
with a tiny pediment and corner acroteria. *HABS*.

Address: North Commerce Street.

Grace Church, *Galena*. 1847–50.

130   This Gothic Revival church is deeply set into the rock hill
      that forms the steep western slope of the city. The rough
      gray stone excavated for the site was used for the walls of
      the church. The architect was C. W. Ottis from Buffalo,
      New York, and his design illustrates the shift from
      neoclassic to neogothic which was initiated with church
      building. The latter style was popularized by, among
      others, Richard Upjohn, who designed the elaborate Grace
      Episcopal Church in Providence, Rhode Island, the patron
      church for the initial Galena congregation, established
      in 1835.

      The sanctuary was deepened considerably in the 1894
      remodeling by William LeBaron Jenney. Also at this time,
      the unstable wooden spire was removed and a crenellated
      parapet in limestone added to finish off the belfry
      stage. *HABS*.

Address: Prospect Street.

Dowling House, *Galena*. 1847.

132   The plan of the James Dowling House is a formal one that is often seen in Georgian examples of a century earlier: a center hallway runs from front to back, containing a U-shaped stair, two chimneys balanced on each exterior side wall, four second-story bedrooms, and a kitchen ell extending to the rear with servants rooms above. The exterior of the Dowling House, however, expresses the full absorption of the Classical Revival: a magnificent Ionic portico graces the attenuated proportions of the façade; a recessed and cantilevered cast-iron balcony serves the front two bedrooms. The column capitals and other woodwork were brought up the river from St. Louis by boat. The architect-builder of this house is unknown. *HABS.*

Address: 120 North Bench Street.

Street view of Dowling House
Drawing of Ionic capital

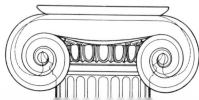

Post Office, *Galena*. 1856–58.

134   In 1826 a post office, the first in northern Illinois, was
established in Galena. In subsequent years the prosperity
of the town justified this substantial government
building which was designed in Washington. Plans for this
and for similar buildings were produced in the office of the
Supervising Architect of the Treasury. The incumbent
architect at this time was Ammi B. Young (1798–1874),
who held the appointment from 1852 to 1860, busy years
for custom houses and post offices. Young was born in
New Hampshire and may have been a pupil of Alexander
Parris. He did much work in Boston before going to
Washington. The Galena Post Office design follows
generally classical lines without committing itself to
stringent classicism.

Address: Greene and Commerce Streets.

Grant House, *Galena.* 1857.

136   This two-story brick house was presented to General
        Ulysses S. Grant by the citizens of Galena after the Civil
        War. Grant had previously lived in Galena, and it was
        fitting that he return to his adopted city. The house was
        originally built and owned by Alexander Jackson, an
        influential citizen of Galena.

        Upon his election to the presidency in 1868, Grant left to
        serve two terms in Washington, returning to Galena in
        1877, but leaving again soon for foreign travel. In 1880 he
        again bid for the Presidential nomination, but lost to
        Garfield. Grant spent his last years in New York, where he
        died in 1885.

        The Grant House is maintained as a state memorial and is
        furnished with possessions of the Grant family. *HABS.*

Address: Bouthiller and Fourth Streets.

Old Main, Knox College, *Galesburg*. 1856.

138 Knox College was chartered in 1837 primarily for the purpose of training missionaries. It was part of a master plan conceived by George Washington Gale, a Presbyterian minister from Oneida, New York, who planned his community of Galesburg as a center for what he hoped to be prosperous farm country. However, it was the coming of the railroad in 1854 that provided financial stability for the city and college.

Old Main, the oldest building on the campus, is a spirited example of Gothic Revival. It is composed of vigorous vertical elements made more emphatic by projecting crenellated towers. The material used is red brick with limestone trim.

In 1858 a fifth debate between Stephen A. Douglas and Abraham Lincoln was held outside this building. Extensively restored, it became a National Historic Landmark in 1962.

Old Unitarian Church, *Geneva*. 1843 and 1855.

140   The modesty of most early Illinois buildings must be
        remembered when one is faced with ambitious and
        exceptional examples. This simple church is the oldest
        Unitarian church building west of New York. It was built in
        part by contributions from Unitarians in Boston and
        Roxbury and was dedicated January 24, 1844. The land
        cost only $22 and the builders, L. and D. Howard, were
        paid $225 for their efforts. The original building was a third
        smaller than the present enlarged one and had neither
        belfry nor vestibule. Both the original building and the
        1855 extension are of native rubble stone twenty inches
        thick. Cement stucco now covers the exterior. The roof
        span of only thirty feet is achieved with a simple oak
        truss with oak purlins and rafters. None of the original
        inside fixtures remain. One may assume that the original
        façade was similar to the four pilaster strips and pediment
        now seen. *HABS*.

Address: Second and James Streets.

North Shore Congregation Israel Synagogue, *Glencoe*. 1964.

142 A reaction in the 1950's against the rectilinear, severe forms of modern architecture resulted in structural experimentation with reinforced concrete shells. The possibility of molding walls and roofs in one piece, the possibility of curvilinear structures creating sculptural space, became a reality. In this synagogue, the architect, Minoru Yamasaki (1912–   ), intelligently combined this new structural freedom with the discipline established earlier in the modern period. The result is a seductively elegant canopy of liquid grace, recalling Art Nouveau decoration, but here extended to express an integral structural concept.

The scheme for the sanctuary consists of eight pairs of reinforced concrete fan vault shells, cast in place with Fiberglas forms. One is reminded of plants like the palm and the calla lily. Each of these sixteen shells is anchored only at its slender base and is stabilized by touching adjacent shells along the flank, and its opposite member at the roof ridge. The intervening spaces are glazed with amber glass. The skylight portion is double glazed and conceals artificial lighting. The height is fifty feet and the span is eighty feet. The execution of the design is of the highest quality.

Address: 1185 Sheridan Road.

Interior view
Rear view of the synagogue

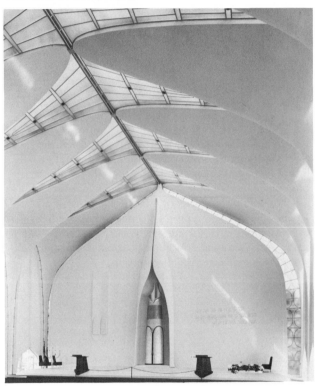

Scott, Foresman and Company Building, *Glenview*. 1966.

144 Industry and commerce have become the primary patrons of architecture in the twentieth century. Commissions from the church, government, and private wealthy individuals no longer hold the importance they once had. It should not be assumed, however, that this shift of patronage has resulted in uniform mediocrity. On the contrary, buildings commissioned by industry and commerce frequently rank among the best architecture of our time.

An example of this quality is the Scott, Foresman and Company Building. It is a complex of four separated units linked together in a landscaped setting. The result is a tranquil, almost campus-like environment appropriate to the work of this publisher of educational materials. The buildings are of reinforced concrete faced with panels of brick and precast concrete. Color-anodized aluminum has been used for window and door frames. The architects were The Perkins and Will Partnership.

Address: 1900 East Lake Avenue.

Corner detail
General view of the buildings

Congregational Church, *Godfrey*. 1854.

146   Godfrey is the site of Monticello College and Preparatory
School for Girls, founded in 1835. One of the first
institutions west of the Alleghenies to offer advanced
education to women, Monticello was established by a
retired Cape Cod sea captain, Benjamin Godfrey. The
church, originally known as the Church of Christ at
Monticello, was built by the joint efforts of the college and
community and was shared by both. Its bell was cast in
Troy, New York, in 1857, and shipped by water to nearby
Alton and from there hauled to Monticello on Captain
Godfrey's ox-cart.

The combination of an essentially Gothic spire with a
classical portico is not at all uncommon in American
architecture. The English were particularly fond of it during
the Baroque period in the seventeenth and eighteenth
centuries, and there are beautiful examples by Christopher
Wren and James Gibbs. American churches emulated such
spires, usually simplifying the design as seen in this
handsome example at Godfrey. Nothing is known of the
architect beyond a record of 1854 mentioning "the partial
completion of a church under contract by W. H.
Howell." *HABS*.

Address: U. S. Route 67.

Deere House, *Grand Detour.* 1836.

148   In 1834 the town of Grand Detour was laid out by Leonard Andrus and named for the ox-bow bend in the Rock River. Two years later, John Deere, a Vermont blacksmith, moved west to seek better fortune and settled in this new community. Deere built the original portion of his wood frame house and lived here until his departure for Moline in 1847. The original house, suggesting plain New England design, measured only 18 feet by 24 feet and was divided into five rooms with two bedrooms upstairs. In the 1921 restoration a front portico and a side fireplace chimney were added. It is maintained as a memorial museum and is a record of pioneer life in Illinois.

Close by is the excavated foundation of the John Deere blacksmith shop where he invented and built the first successful steel plow. The sticky soil of the Midwest made the cast-iron plow impractical for farming. Leonard Andrus, founder of Grand Detour, was once associated with Deere in the plow business.

St. Peter's Church, *Grand Detour,* 1849–50.

150   In the 1840's the Gothic Revival began to assert itself as a popular choice. Episcopalians were especially partial to it for their churches and colleges. Although the architectural demands of Gothic in the full sense of that style were beyond the purses and skills of the early settlers, even a diluted expression was a respite from the ubiquitous neoclassic.

This pleasant and diminutive example, only 24 feet by 45 feet over-all, is of rough fieldstone fitted with a wood belfry and spire. With the advent of the railroads, which passed Grand Detour by, the town declined and the church was closed for fifty years. It was repaired for use again in the early twentieth century.

Grand Detour was the site of a French trading center. By 1840 the prosperous village on the peninsula included several stores and blacksmith shops, a wagon factory, a sawmill, a flour mill, and a cradle factory. *HABS.*

Illinois Farm. *Havana.*

152 Characteristic of the Illinois landscape are its clusters of farm buildings on the flat prairie. While the individual buildings are usually without architectural distinction, the informal grouping of house, barns, silo, and often trees, make an attractive feature in the countryside. This farm complex near Havana has been chosen as representative.

Address: West of Havana on U.S. Route 136.

Beecher Hall, Illinois College, *Jacksonville*. 1829–30.

154 This building housed one of the state's earliest colleges
(1829). Belief in the value of education was strong in the
pioneer; the early settlements of Illinois contained a
surprising number of well-educated people who naturally
became leaders in establishing institutions. The Rev. John
M. Ellis was prominent in the founding of Illinois College.
A $10,000 donation solicited by seven young men called
the Yale Band substantially aided its beginning. Their
organization, named the Illinois Association, established
some fifteen colleges in the Midwest. Dr. Edward Beecher,
the first president of the college, for whom this building is
named, came from the famous family which included
the preacher, Henry Ward Beecher, and the author,
Harriet Beecher Stowe.

Beecher Hall was built in two stages, of similar designs,
suggesting the late Georgian style of New England rather
than the newer Classical Revival. Semicircular windows,
Adam-like interior details, the Flemish bond of the brick,
and dormer windows (now removed) contribute to
this impression. Plans were drawn by a local carpenter and
joiner, James Kerr. It is uncertain whether a portico was
part of the original plan, but an early photograph shows
one whose design is that of about 1840. The present
portico was built in 1928.

The building has served a variety of college purposes:
professor's house, library, classroom, and science
laboratory. Its attic rooms were used for the first medical
courses given in the state. *HABS.*

Kornthal Church, near *Jonesboro*. 1860.

156   This church was built by families of the Lutheran faith who immigrated from Austria to this country in 1852–53. Landing at New Orleans, the immigrants came up the Mississippi by flatboat to Willard's Landing, near the present town of Ware. Traveling a few miles eastward, they settled in a fertile valley which they called Kornthal, meaning "valley of grain." The community was never incorporated as a village, but at one time it included a church, a church school and parsonage, a box factory, a gristmill, a country store and a distillery. The church is the only remaining building.

The planning of the church, dedicated to St. Paul, was begun soon after the settlement was made, and a typical Austrian *Betsaal* (house of prayer) design was used. In Austria at that time Protestant churches were not allowed spires, nor were they permitted to have doors opening on the street. This plain frame rectangular church was built with side doors and no steeple. The front entrance, steeple, and bell tower were added in 1889.

The interior of the church is tiny but impressive. The high pulpit, its steep stair, and the baptismal font are all examples of peasant handicraft. Charles Fettinger, one of the original Austrian settlers, is credited with designing and executing the church. Ernest Kollehner is recorded as the builder of the steeple. *HABS.*

Address: Two and one-half miles south of Jonesboro on Route 127.

Side view of the church
Decorative pulpit

Jubilee College, Jubilee College State Park (near *Peoria*). 1839.

158 Founding colleges in the wilderness was the mission of the Rev. Philander Chase. In 1824 he founded Kenyon College at Gambier, Ohio, and in 1839, Jubilee College at Robin's Nest, Illinois. For twenty-two years, from 1840 to 1862, Jubilee College flourished as one of the earliest educational enterprises in the state.

It contained a theological department, a college proper, a boy's preparatory school, and a girl's seminary. Its major building combined chapel, classrooms, and dormitory, and is built of yellow sandstone. The Gothic style is conveyed with lancet windows, latticed panes, and recessed portals. As in Kenyon College, Bishop Chase thought Gothic was appropriate to his endeavors, and his choice followed the first use of collegiate Gothic in 1832 at New York University, designed by Town and Davis. Apart from suggesting sectarian sponsorship, the use of the Gothic style for college buildings had precedent in the early colleges of Oxford and Cambridge. The associational value of an architectural style is a powerful one and none of us is wholly free from its influence.

Three times after the Civil War the school was reopened, but without lasting success. In 1933 the college and grounds overlooking the valley of Kickapoo Creek were presented to the State of Illinois by Dr. George A. Zeller as a permanent memorial. In the Jubilee churchyard, marked by a stone lectern, is the grave of Bishop Chase, for seventeen years the first bishop of the Illinois diocese of the Protestant Episcopal Church. *HABS.*

Address: North of U.S. 150 about fifteen miles northwest of Peoria.

Jubilee College buildings today
Original grouping of college buildings

Hickox House, *Kankakee*. 1900.

In 1900 Frank Lloyd Wright arrived at a solution for small house design which became a basis for his work for a decade. The characteristics of this prairie house design were a cruciform plan, horizontally banded windows, and emphatic roof forms whose projecting eaves echoed the flat midwestern landscape.

The debut of the prairie house took place in Kankakee in 1900 with the building of two adjacent houses, the B. Harley Bradley and the Warren Hickox houses, although two projects by Wright for prairie type designs had appeared a few months earlier in the *Ladies Home Journal*. The interiors of these houses are at once spacious and snug. The bold geometry characteristic of Wright shows up in the dark wood and light stucco exterior of the Hickox house. There is also the suggestion of modern medievalism in the use of casement windows and gabled roof forms which link Wright with the Queen Anne style of Norman Shaw and Charles F. A. Voysey in England. Behind them all stands William Morris whose pervasive influence runs like a red thread through the early history of modern design down to the present.

Address: 687 South Harrison Avenue.

Joseph Sears School, *Kenilworth*. 1912.

162 George W. Maher (1864–1926) can be numbered among
the architects strongly influenced by Louis Sullivan and
Frank Lloyd Wright. The simple forms and respect for
materials common in the architecture of this midwest band
was inspired by William Morris, the English leader of the
Arts and Crafts movement.

Maher himself was strongly oriented to the work of
Sullivan, and his designs frequently stress that symmetry
and ornament peculiar to Sullivan. An example of
George Maher's work is the Joseph Sears School. It shows
his preference for large areas of brick work and a
somewhat conservative façade.

Address: 542 Abbotsford Road.

Old Knox County Courthouse, *Knoxville*. 1837–40.

164 A splendid example of the Greek Doric style applied to
civic architecture is this former courthouse of Knox
County. Its architect was John Mandeville (1815–59) who
was only twenty-two and recently arrived from Bergen,
New Jersey, when he designed the building. It replaced
an inadequate log courthouse which stood elsewhere on
the village green. The county commissioners were so
satisfied with their new structure, they voted an additional
expenditure of $750 for a cupola. This afterthought was
soon removed, however, because it was without
supporting internal structure and its weight was pushing
the side walls outward. The walls are of red brick,
originally painted a cream color. The portico columns are
also of brick with the fluting of plaster. The lintels are of
stone. The Doric entablature and roof structure are of
wood. In the early 1870's a cast-iron stairway was added
to the portico, thus providing a main entrance and exit to
the second-story courtroom and offices, and releasing the
original north vestibule for additional office space. When
Galesburg became the county seat in 1873, the building
was remodeled into an opera house with an auditorium
on the second floor. The courthouse now serves as a
municipal building and as the Knox County Museum.

Standing west of the courthouse is the former Hall of
Records, built in 1854 and also designed by Mandeville.
Its floors were covered with steel plate and the windows
were supplied with heavy metal shutters inside, an early
conception of fireproof construction. The building is
now the public library. *HABS*.

Old Knox County Jail, *Knoxville.* 1841–45.

166   This jail combines a rear cell block with the jailor's living quarters in front. We know its designer was Zelotes Cooley who, with Alvah Wheeler, built the nearby courthouse. It is constructed half of stone, half of brick, with a wood-framed kitchen ell at the side.

The design of this jail is distinguished particularly by the solitary confinement cells on the first floor of the cell block. If Illinois ever had a Bastille, this is it. The great size of each stone used to construct the cell block was an excessive load even with only one per wagon, and this may account in part for the four years required for its completion. The builder's ingenuity is artfully expressed in the cell-door security arrangement, which provides a lock far from the most extended reach of the prisoner. The second story of the cell block is divided into two large rooms or "bull pens" for local inebriates and tramps.

Living quarters for the jailor or sheriff comprise the two-story front portion of the jail adjoining the cell block and afford a sharp contrast in comfort. The present-day housewife might object, however, to the vagrants using the same stairs to reach the second-story cells that she had to use to reach her sleeping rooms. *HABS.*

Address: North Market Street.

St. Mary's Chapel. *Knoxville.* 1881–88.

168   This chapel was once a part of a Protestant Episcopal girls' school which opened in the spring of 1868. The chapel and an astronomical observatory are the only remains of this once flourishing school, which succumbed to changing educational preferences and the economic depression of the 1930's.

A fire in 1883 burned all except the unfinished chapel and observatory. A new school building (now gone) was attached to the chapel by a cloister (ca. 1890), part of which exists as an arcaded porch to the building. An ambitious and impressive Gothic design has been used for the chapel, whose steep roof is supported by wood trusses within. Also impressive are the stained-glass windows, some of which are of European origin and some of the finest from American studios. In 1888 an altar of Caen stone with panels of tinted alabaster was installed.

Address: Douglas Street.

Exterior view
Arcaded porch of chapel

Poole House, *Lake Bluff.* 1914.

170   The style of Louis XV in architecture and furniture design is
       known for its intimate scale and comfort, well suited to
       domestic life. It was a reaction against the stiffness and
       grandeur of the style of Louis XIV and, in this sense, can
       be said to be the beginning of modern residential design.
       The appeal of the eighteenth-century French manner is
       continued in this twentieth-century adaptation by David
       Adler (1882–1949). For Ralph H. Poole, Adler designed
       a pleasantly formal house of stucco with a slate mansard
       roof. It was Adler's first country house commission.
       As is characteristic of the eighteenth-century prototypes,
       the orders are not used, and instead the corners are
       picked out by quoins playing the role of pilasters. The chief
       elements are the generously large window openings
       headed with segmental curves. Stretched across the garden
       façade are five major rooms with doors *en filade*.

       Adler was an architect of education and taste, versatile
       in his knowledge of styles and capable of fresh solutions
       within a traditional framework. From the beginning of his
       career, after architecture study at Princeton and the
       Paris Ecole des Beaux Arts, Adler specialized in residential
       work. Examples of his architecture are found on the
       east and west coasts as well as in Chicago and on the
       North Shore.

Market Square, *Lake Forest*. 1916.

Howard Shaw (1869–1926) was an outstanding architect of the Midwest. His wide practice included various types of buildings, and he was particularly interested in garden design. Shaw studied at Yale University and at M.I.T. This training, together with foreign travel, prepared him for a career in architecture which was noted for its highly refined though traditional designs.

Among his works is this attractive shopping center of 1916, laid out as a U-shaped group of stores with apartments above. A covered walkway connects some of the stores. Monotony is avoided by units which vary in design and materials. Brick with limestone, stucco, and half-timbering are used. The visual effect suggests Flanders or Germany of the Middle Ages, but there is no copying. Two towers, a fountain, and a landscaped mall are part of the total design. The simple medievalism of this well-scaled composition recalls similar city planning efforts in England in the early twentieth century. Shaw was assisted by the noted planner, Edward H. Bennett (1874–1954).

This shopping center replaced an earlier drab business district. Of this project, architect Peter B. Wight wrote, "As far as we know this is the first time in America that the *center of a town* has been taken and replanned and rebuilt, not as an altruistic or charitable undertaking, but in order to produce good practical as well as aesthetic effects."

McKendree College Chapel, *Lebanon*. 1856–58.

174   Situated on a forested campus is this chapel building of McKendree College, founded in 1828, the oldest Methodist college in the Midwest. The chapel proper is located on the lofty second floor with the ground floor given over to offices and other uses. The building is a late example of restrained classical styling. The brick façade is marked with brick pilasters and a beautiful wood doorway. When built, it was the largest building of its kind in Illinois; it seated slightly more than four hundred persons.

Originally the building was surmounted by a wood belfry and spire which rose 145 feet. The spire was topped with a gilded globe, three feet in diameter, and an outsized weathervane. Active plans are underway to restore this Lebanon landmark. *HABS.*

Four Bottle Tavern, *Lee Center.* ca. 1845.

176 This two-story frame house was built between 1840 and
1850 as indicated by its construction. It stands west of
the village of Lee Center, which was laid out in 1846. The
house occupies the site of an earlier tavern kept by
Benjamin Whittaker in 1839. This early tavern drew
travelers of the old Chicago-Galena stage road. Its upstairs
was arranged with a ballroom across the entire front.
The doorway details are especially fine. Fluted pilasters,
dentils, and a rope moulding are used. *HABS.*

Address: North side of Chicago Road, east of Clinton Street

University Hall, Lincoln College, *Lincoln*. 1865.

178   University Hall is the oldest structure on the campus of
      Lincoln College. The groundbreaking ceremony on
      February 12, 1865, marked the start of the first institution
      of learning to be named after the President. The college
      was originally sponsored by the Presbyterians.

      In design, University Hall illustrates the newly arrived
      Victorian style with traces of the nearly vanished Classical
      Revival. The three-storied red brick structure rests on a
      high foundation of Joliet limestone. Located on the
      highest spot on the campus, the building's square cupola
      stands as a beacon in this area. The architect of University
      Hall was George W. Gayle.

Rogers House, *Marengo*. 1849.

180   Many of the early settlers in Illinois were from New
       England, and similarities between buildings there and
       in Illinois have been noted. The design of the Anson
       Rogers House, one of two identical houses on the same
       road, seems remarkably like many of the cottages of
       the Maine coast. Neoclassic designs were carried westward
       in handbooks of instruction intended for carpenter-
       builders. Edward Shaw's *Rural Architecture* may have
       provided the source for the Rogers House. *HABS*.

Address: U.S. Route 20 south of Marengo.

Cloud State Bank, *McLeansboro*. 1881.

Records tell us that the Cloud State Bank was designed by its owner, Chalon G. Cloud, who started his banking business in 1871 and completed his new building in the spring of 1882. A contemporary description refers to it as handsome and elegant as any building in southern Illinois. In 1924 it became the People's National Bank, which now uses it as a directors' room.

It is representative of the florid Second Empire style that crossed the Atlantic from France and found its way into vernacular American Victorian practice. When the Louvre was enlarged in 1852–57 under Napoleon III, it initiated a loosely interpreted revival of the French Renaissance style of the late sixteenth century as seen in the original Louvre-Tuileries complex. Three of its characteristic features were frequently used in the nineteenth-century version: the square dome, the mansard roof, and the banded column. Evidence of this style can be seen in all the leading cities of Europe.

Some may dismiss such an example as the Cloud State Bank as architectural millinery, but none will deny its vigor. Its red and white color and assemblage of architectural motifs make it a splendid example of American neobaroque.

Address: Washington Street.

Old Woodford County Courthouse, *Metamora*.
1844–46.

When Metamora became the county seat in 1843, the ·
building committee approved a courthouse design similar
to the one at Lacon in adjacent Marshall County. This
Greek Revival scheme was standard for modest temples
of justice built at the time to serve newly established
counties. A subcontractor named David Irving was
responsible for the construction of the courthouse. The
brick was locally made and the timber felled nearby, much
of it black walnut which was then in abundant supply.
The ground floor provided offices divided by a central
corridor. A rear stairway led to the courtroom on the
second floor. In 1870 these stairs were moved to the
outside front of the building and the arrangement of the
courtroom altered. Two wings were added about 1884.
When the county seat was transferred to Eureka in 1896,
the building was used by the village. Removal of the
outside stairs and the wings have restored the courthouse
to its original exterior appearance.

Woodford County was part of the old Eighth Circuit and
Abraham Lincoln regularly pleaded cases at Metamora
between 1843 and 1857. Old Woodford County
Courthouse and the courthouse at Mount Pulaski are the
only two remaining courthouses in which Lincoln
practiced law. Other men of prominence who attended
court at Metamora were Adlai E. Stevenson, later vice-
president; David Davis, later Supreme Court justice;
and Robert.G. Ingersoll, famous scholar and orator.

In 1921 the building became a state memorial and museum
devoted to Lincoln and pioneer life. The restored
courtroom contains some of the original furnishings.

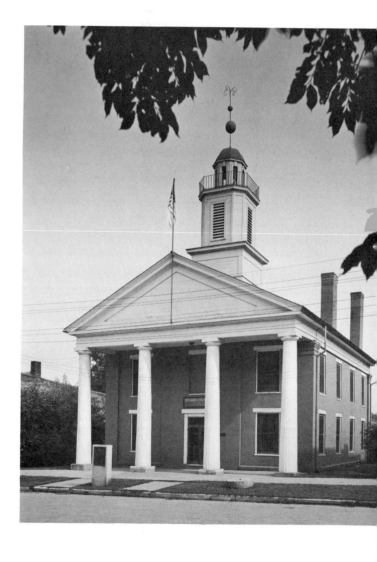

Deere and Company Administrative Center, *Moline*.
1962–64.

The prestige corporation-headquarters office-building
placed in a suburban setting is an often encountered
assignment in post-World War II architecture. Nowhere
has the problem been more effectively and beautifully
solved as in this example at Moline by Eero Saarinen
(1910–62) and Associates.

Its basic scheme is a slender eight-story block set in
a landscaped ravine overlooking two small lakes, one
of which serves as a cooling pond for the building's
airconditioning system. The discipline associated with steel
framing is everywhere evident and is made more
expressive, more dramatic, by extended trellis-like sun
screens. The handsome dark brown color of the oxidizing
special-alloy steel, together with the play of filtered light
across the façade, gives a richness and depth to the
structure not seen in earlier antiseptic and flat designs.

This distinguished building was cited for excellence and
innovation in design by the American Institute of
Architects in 1965. One of Eero Saarinen's last works, its
quality is probably unsurpassed by any of his earlier
buildings.

Address: John Deere Road.

Exterior view from entrance drive
Detail of sun screen

Allerton House, Robert Allerton Park, near
Monticello. 1899.

188   Renewed interest in colonial Georgian buildings in
America was initiated by the architectural firm of McKim,
Mead and White in the early 1880's. The work of these
eastern architects did much to establish the popularity of
the Georgian revival, and the Robert Allerton House
can be traced to this influence. Its architect, John Borie,
was perhaps more strongly influenced by English country
houses of the late seventeenth century than by the more
modest American examples. He and the owner studied
European examples of houses and landscaped parks before
settling on the design of this house and its grounds.

The house is set in an extensive park covering fifteen
hundred acres, through which flows the Sangamon River.
Immediately adjacent to the house are a series of
gardens, both formal and informal, which incorporate
many pieces of sculpture and garden ornaments.

The house and its park were given to the University of
Illinois in 1946. The park is open to the public.

Address: Four miles southwest of Monticello on Ill. 47.

Appellate Court Building, *Mount Vernon*. 1854.

190 In 1848 a new constitution provided that the Supreme
Court should sit in three areas or divisions. Mount Vernon
was chosen for the Southern or First Division, and in
1854, with a $6,000 appropriation, this building was begun.
An additional appropriation of $10,000 was needed to
finish the building according to the original plan, whose
architect is unknown. The constitution of 1870 established
appellate courts and both courts shared this building until
1897 when the Supreme Court was centered in Springfield.

The initial plan was rectangular, with north and south
wings, converting the plan to a Greek cross, added in
1874. The structure is of painted brick with simple pilaster
strips around it and a wood cornice. The elegance of
the façade is set by paired Ionic columns in wood and
a double curved stairway leading to lofty main rooms on
the second floor. The cast-iron stair was manufactured
in St. Louis. The refinement of this façade suggests an
architect from that city. *HABS.*

Address: Fourteenth and West Main Streets.

Young House, *Nauvoo.* 1840.

192   Brigham Young was one of Joseph Smith's closest
       associates, and he became the leader of the Mormon
       Church in Utah after Smith's murder in 1844. Pressured by
       anti-Mormon violence, he led an exodus from Nauvoo
       in February, 1846, and was the principal organizer of a
       permanent and prosperous community in Utah.

       Vermont-born Brigham Young was a carpenter and builder
       and was active in the erection of the Kirtland Temple in
       Kirtland, Ohio, built between 1832 and 1836 under the
       direct supervision of Joseph Smith. It is uncertain whether
       he participated in the building of the Temple at Nauvoo
       (1841–45), or even in the building of the house bearing his
       name. The house was originally of symmetrical design, a
       center two-story portion flanked by single-story wings. It
       is built of handmade brick and rests on a native stone
       foundation. Stone sills and lintels were originally used
       throughout. *HABS.*

       Address: Sixth and Kimball Streets.

Brigham Young House
Stone capital from destroyed Nauvoo Temple

Mansion House, *Nauvoo.* 1841.

194   The sparsely occupied portion of Nauvoo called "the Flat" was once the center of the populous Mormon city founded by Joseph Smith. The prophet and organizer of the Mormon Church arrived in Quincy, Illinois, in the winter of 1838–39 fleeing persecution by the Missourians across the Mississippi. Aided by sympathetic citizens of Quincy, the Mormons settled fifty miles north at a place called Commerce, soon renamed Nauvoo, and obtained a city charter from the General Assembly in 1840. In a few years Nauvoo became the largest city in Illinois (more than fifteen hundred inhabitants).

The Mansion House was the second home of Joseph Smith. Nearby stands the Homestead, built of logs, the first home of the Smith family in Nauvoo. The Mansion House is a large frame building with clapboards. Its front is visually framed with four broad pilasters. Small dentil mouldings ornament the center doorway, lower window frames, and the cornice. The many rooms of the Mansion House provided Mormon hospitality, and it was once used as a hotel. The hotel wing was torn down in the late 1880's or early 1890's. The house is now maintained as a museum by the Reorganized Church of Jesus Christ of Latter Day Saints, Independence, Missouri. *HABS.*

Address: Main and Water Streets.

Ivins-Babbitt House, *Nauvoo*. 1842.

196 The persistence of Georgian architectural style into the nineteenth century is evident in the characteristic five-bay window arrangement of the Ivins-Babbitt House. The plan consists of a small center stairhall with a single room on either side and an ell to the rear. The Federalist style (Georgian tempered by the neo-classical) is seen in the center doorway and in a deep wooden cornice with dentils. This cornice unclassically receives five attic windows, a free American adaptation. In Georgian architecture such windows would be treated as dormers. The bricks are sand-molded, salmon-colored, and laid in Flemish bond pattern. These bricks bear the imprint of Isaac Hill, a professional brick maker who operated the Law Brick Yard in 1842 at Nauvoo. The foundations, sills, and lintels are of native stone.

This house was the home of James Ivins, a convert to Mormonism from New Jersey, who purchased this lot from Joseph Smith in 1842. Three years later Elias Smith bought the house and the two flanking brick buildings on the site, one of which remains. In this complex he lived and managed a post office and print shop from which was published the *Times & Seasons*. John Taylor, editor of this periodical and the town newspaper, once shared this house with Smith. With the migration of the Mormons in 1846, the house was occupied by Almon W. Babbitt, who was one of the three trustees who sold most of the Mormon property at Nauvoo. The river flat once contained approximately 500 homes of which fewer than fifty remain. *HABS*.

Address: Main and Kimball Streets.

New Trier West High School, *Northfield*. 1965–67.

198   The design of this high school suggests the campus plan associated with colleges and universities. A central library and administration unit is connected to three separate academic classroom buildings by corridors at the ground level and also by bridged passageways at the third level. Two additional buildings, one for music, drama, and speech, and one housing boys and girls gymnasiums, are linked by ground-level corridors to these units as well. The resulting courtyard is excavated and the fill is banked against the exterior walls of the connecting corridors providing a main entrance at the second level.

The spaciousness of the plan relieves congestion, and the rooms provided encourage variety and high quality education in a changing academic world. The exterior is of red-face brick and exposed concrete framing. The architectural detailing and the mechanical services of the building have been skillfully coordinated. The Perkins and Will Partnership and The Architects Collaborative were the two associated firms for this high school.

Address: Happ Road.

Telephone Switching Center, *Norway*. 1961.

200 The manmade landscape of the twentieth century is being changed by radical structures which are demanded by our technological age. Such an example is the American Telephone and Telegraph regional switching center at Norway. It serves as a major link in the nation's com- munication network and is one of several such centers across the country. It also serves as a junction station along key radio and cable routes. The center is a two-story reinforced concrete building designed to house complex electronic equipment. Adjacent to the structure is an eight-legged tower standing 227 feet high which supports 18 antennae.

Address: Twenty miles northeast of Ottawa on U.S. Route 52.

Wright House and Studio, *Oak Park*. 1889 and 1895.

202 This is the first house that Frank Lloyd Wright (1867–1959) built for himself. It is in the informal Queen Anne shingle style, not unlike designs by his first employer, architect Joseph Lyman Silsbee. It is particularly related to the eastern work of Bruce Price and the English work of Norman Shaw. Although Wright's personal style is not yet revealed here, the house illustrates the simplified medievalism which was characteristic of his formative period.

It was in this house that Wright started his independent architectural career with a number of "bootleg" houses, while still employed by Louis Sullivan. Later, in 1895, Wright designed a studio addition on the corner lot facing Chicago Avenue, which housed his growing practice and the young draftsmen who participated in the first mature phase of his work lasting to 1909. The architecture of the studio itself is an indication of the rapid transformation of Wright's architecture within several years.

Address: 428 Forest Avenue; studio: 951 Chicago Avenue.

Unity Temple, *Oak Park*. 1905–7.

Religious architecture is by nature conservative and slow to change. But Frank Lloyd Wright, in his spirited unorthodoxy, persuaded the Unitarian parish of Oak Park to forego a steeple pointing upward and to accept a skylight letting light shine downward, dramatizing the separateness of the congregation from the outside world.

In Unity Temple, Wright manipulated the geometry of the square and cube into a compact and largely opaque design. The plan is faultless: two major elements, church and parish house, are connected by an entrance link. The composition is remarkably compact yet provides for separateness of functions. For the church proper, Wright developed a central square plan into a Greek cross, whose arms provide seating balconies, and returned the plan to a square by filling out the four corners with stairway towers. Like the music of Bach, the achitecture of Wright develops magnificent variations on simple themes.

Not the least of Wright's achievement is his use of poured concrete, which was visible in the original aggregate surface of the exterior. Unity Temple is the first monumentally expressed use of concrete in architecture. *HABS*.

Address: Lake Street and Kenilworth Avenue.

Exterior view
Interior of the meeting hall

First National Bank of Shawneetown, *Old Shawneetown*. 1836.

206   Despite the naïve use of an odd number of columns across the façade and the incorrect combination of a Greek Doric temple placed on a Roman temple base, this Classical Revival bank shows great refinement in its details. The unknown architect was obviously learned in classical architecture. The end columns are more closely spaced and are inclined inward one inch following the optical corrections seen in ancient Greek examples. The designer has managed an interesting side stair whose top platform is supported by a single Doric column. His design of wrought-iron railings is also notable. The stone used resembles travertine in color and texture; however, as a practical man, the architect has substituted more economical brick for the side walls. Also, he has squeezed a fourth floor out of the entablature portion of his temple bank, whose windows occur only on the sides away from the street-corner view.

Address: Main and Cross Streets.

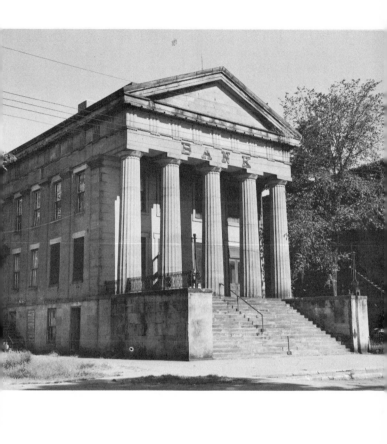

208   The formation of a new county in 1840 made necessary this courthouse whose scheme followed the then current prototype of temple portico with cupola above. It is similar to the slightly earlier courthouse at Knoxville. Variation in cupola design was the limited opportunity for individualism offered by Classical Revival courthouses which otherwise form a monotonous series.

Before the advent of bureaucracy, governmental buildings were simple affairs. This courthouse has a center hallway dividing the lower floor into symmetrical office spaces for the county and circuit clerks, the recorder, and the county judge. The second floor consists of but one big courtroom which now has none of the original furniture. There have been a number of additions and alterations. In 1905 the circular brick columns were stuccoed over and the original wood shingles were replaced.

The architect is unknown, but he may have been one Abner Hebbard who arrived in Oquawka in 1842 and was listed as an architect by trade in a local partnership making furniture. *HABS.*

Address: Fourth and Warren Streets.

Hossack House, *Ottawa*. 1854–55.

210   The inventive design of the John Hossack House illustrates
       the variations that occurred within the Greek Revival. The
       architect has used continuous porches across the two main
       fronts, but neither follows the conventional classical
       temple motif. The rear portico, which overlooks the
       Illinois River, is arcaded and supported on high square
       piers. The entrance portico opposite is arranged in two
       stories with a latticed wood railing for the second-story
       porch. A center hallway divides a pair of major rooms on
       either side. Originally small symmetrical wings flanked
       the central block, one a kitchen and the other probably
       an office.

       Little is known of the Chicago architect, Sylvanus Grow.
       John Hossack was born in Scotland, became wealthy in
       the grain trade in Ottawa and Chicago, was a staunch
       abolitionist, and, according to family tradition, had
       specific ideas about the design of his house. *HABS*.

Address: 210 West Prospect Avenue.

Arcaded portico facing river
Entrance front with double-storied portico

Lakeview Center for the Arts and Sciences, *Peoria*. 1964–65.

212   The recent popularity of art centers and science museums has resulted in the establishment of new institutions and the building of new facilities for exhibits and community activities. An illustration is the Lakeview Center for the Arts and Sciences which opened in March, 1965, after a decade of planning. Its program includes an art gallery, an art school, a history and nature museum, and a planetarium. Facilities for each have been planned in the center which was designed by Victor Gruen (1903–   ) Associates. In design it represents a departure from the monumental schemes that formerly characterized museum architecture.

Address: 1125 West Lake Avenue.

Exterior view of the Center
Detail

New Salem Village, near *Petersburg*. Rebuilt as of *ca.* 1835.

214   The village of New Salem was settled in 1828 and had a brief existence of about ten years, during which time its population never reached three hundred inhabitants. It rapidly declined after the transfer of the Menard County seat to Petersburg in 1839. Abandoned for decades, it was not until 1906, with the purchase of the land by William Randolph Hearst, that interest revived in the site as a memorial to Lincoln's early years.

Abraham Lincoln arrived in New Salem in the summer of 1831, aged twenty-two. He clerked in Offut's grocery store and then served as captain in the Black Hawk War. Returning to New Salem in 1832, he ran unsuccessfully for the state legislature. He won in 1834 and was re-elected two years later. In April, 1837, he left the village for a law partnership in Springfield, eighteen miles away.

The ghost village of New Salem was entirely rebuilt as a historic shrine—the place where Lincoln began his political career. Only the ruins of the Onstot Cooper Shop had survived, and no pictorial record of the town's appearance during Lincoln's time or later was ever made. Nevertheless, the restoration of the log-cabin village gives us a vivid picture of the rudimentary structures that formed early Illinois settlements. Rebuilding began in 1931.

Address: New Salem State Park.

Strauss House, *Pittsfield. ca.* 1842.

216   The use of the lathe and jig saw provided the carpenter-
builder with an opportunity for inventive design. At times
the overdecoration resulted in a style that could only be
described as "carpenter's frenzy." A restrained version of
carpenter decoration is this two-story house with a fanciful
front porch which may have been a later addition. The jig
saw did not come into use until the 1860's, but the use of
the lathe was very common in the earlier part of the
century.

Address: South side of U.S. Routes 36 and 54.

Farnsworth House, *Plano*. 1950.

218 The repose and classicism of Mies van der Rohe's
architecture is illustrated in this country retreat. Char-
acteristically, the architect was unconcerned with rustic
materials or picturesque forms. Instead he has designed
a precise framework of white-painted steel as a pavilion
enclosed entirely with glass. The precision of the structure
is heightened by the contrasting naturalness of the
wooded site.

The diagramatic simplicity of the scheme, roof and floor
planes with eight supporting columns, represents the idea
in architecture of "less is more" pursued by this architect.
The simple is frequently the most difficult. In concept it
foreshadows the principle of reduction in art to the
simplest elements, a principle often seen in contemporary
painting and sculpture. Mies van der Rohe's work empha-
sizes the essential and eliminates the superfluous. The
Farnsworth House conveys that air of finality possessed
only by masterpieces.

Clayville Tavern, *Pleasant Plains. ca.* 1825.

220 This restored Federal-type brick tavern was one of the
stagecoach stops on the Beardstown-Springfield road.
It was built by Moses Broadwell about 1825. According to
an early description, double galleries were built on the
north and south, and evidence of such galleries can be
seen in the vacant holes in the sides of the structure where
supports were once located. The tavern became the
nucleus of a small village consisting of a kiln, smith's shop,
tanyard, store, school, and a few houses.

The place was originally known as the Broadwell Tavern,
but was later called Clayville Tavern when it became the
rallying point for the Whig political party and "Clay's
Men" between 1832 and 1844 when Henry Clay ran twice
for the presidency. A glee club was organized here to
promote Clay's candidacy. On one occasion, a Whig flag
was raised on an "ash pole 100 feet high," and on another
occasion (July 4, 1842) some four hundred people marched
out from Springfield to a patriotic all-day rally and cele-
bration with dinner prepared here for the multitude.
Lincoln was lawyer for the Broadwell family and was a
frequent guest.

Clayville flourished until the railroads put an end to the
stagecoach runs and to the pioneer period as well. In 1960
the deteriorating building was privately purchased and
restored as a public place and museum. *HABS.*

Address: East of Pleasant Plains on Route 125
(twelve miles west of Springfield).

Exterior view of the tavern
Remodeled interior

Fort de Chartres, *Prairie du Rocher*. 1753–56.

The most substantial reminder of French exploration and control of the Mississippi Valley is Fort de Chartres. It was first completed in 1720 as a wooden stockade and named for the son of Phillip II, duke of Orleans and regent of France. It was rebuilt in 1753 of stone quarried from nearby cliffs. The remaining foundations show us a square plan with four corner bastions pointing outward and two opposite gateways. Its walls were originally eighteen feet high and enclosed numerous buildings arranged around a square parade ground. These included a government house, chapel, barracks, kitchen, coach house, and powder magazine. The fort was capable of housing four hundred men, although its garrison rarely exceeded half that number.

Fort de Chartres, the pride of New France, flew the French flag for less than a decade after its completion. With the Treaty of Paris in 1763, all French land east of the Mississippi was ceded to England. The English took possession in 1765 and renamed it Fort Cavendish. This seat of British government in Illinois country lasted only until 1772 when, due to floods, its was abandoned and partially destroyed. In 1913 the site became a state park and was subsequently restored and partially rebuilt. *HABS*.

Creole House, *Prairie du Rocher*. ca. 1800 and ca. 1858.

224   The earlier portion of this house is on the south and is built in the typical French palisade log construction resting on a stone foundation. The north portion was added by a later owner, F. W. Brickey, whose name is locally associated with the house even though he moved on about 1870. Mr. Brickey's north addition is of the newer stud-wall construction, and he also weatherboarded the earlier portion before he moved into it about 1855. This modest house is one of the few remaining examples of the vernacular French building characteristic of this part of the Mississippi Valley. *HABS.*

Florence Hotel, *Pullman* (now part of *Chicago*). 1881.

226   Illinois history has had its share of nineteenth-century
       attempts at utopias, idealized communities, and
       cooperative experiments. A concomitant of many
       schemes was the model town, an architectural
       expression of social harmony.

       This spirit of reform and idealism with a practical purpose
       was seen in George Pullman's creation of a whole new
       town that would supply workers for adjacent factories
       manufacturing his famous sleeping cars. Landscape
       engineer Nathan F. Barrett and architect Solon Spencer
       Beman (1853–1914) were given forty-five hundred acres
       of land on the west shore of Lake Calumet to plan and
       design a model town with those elements of comfort and
       beauty that most of the working class were unaccustomed
       to. A grid street pattern was used, with major buildings
       placed at intersections to relieve the monotony. The archi-
       tectural style was a mixture of Gothic and Queen Anne.

       Among the major buildings were two market houses, an
       ambitious shopping center, a church, a school, and the
       Hotel Florence. Work was begun in 1880. In 1896 Pullman
       was awarded a medal by the Austrian government for
       having founded "the most perfect town in the world."
       HABS.

       Address: 11111 South Forestville.

John Wood House, *Quincy*. 1835.

The first settlement of Quincy dates from 1822 when two log cabins were built by John Wood and Willard Keyes, both newly arrived from the East. In 1825 the city and Adams County of which it is the seat were founded and named for President John Quincy Adams. Wood saw Quincy develop into a major shipping center. Prior to the Civil War it was the second largest city in Illinois. Wood's offices included state senator, governor, and quartermaster general of Illinois in the Civil War.

Since 1907 the John Wood House has been a public museum and home of the Historical Society of Quincy and Adams County. The furnished interiors of this Greek Revival house are a record of Governor Wood and of ante-bellum life in Illinois. The architectural details throughout are especially fine and may have been executed by St. Louis craftsmen. The exterior window frames beyond the portico are ornamented with carvings, and a splendid elliptical window is set within the pediment.

Address: Twelfth Street between State and Kentucky Streets.

Bull House, *Quincy. ca.* 1850.

230   On Maine Street in Quincy one can discover excellent
        examples of Victorian mansions executed in various
        modifications of that fluid style. Among them is the
        Lorenzo Bull mansion, a wood house in a bracketed
        mid-century Mississippi Valley vernacular manner.
        Lorenzo Bull was one of Quincy's pioneer settlers who
        arrived in the spring of 1833 at the age of fourteen. In
        1844 he formed a mercantile partnership with his brother
        Charles and their success became the base of a family
        fortune. Later the brothers sold their business and engaged
        in banking with equal success. The Bull House, now owned
        by the Park District, is occupied by the Women's City Club.

        At the rear of the site (1515 Jersey Street) is the Lorenzo
        Bull Carriage House of the same date. It is a charming
        design with vertical siding, free from any commitment to
        a particular architectural style. The carriage house is now
        occupied by the Quincy Art Center.

Address: 1550 Maine Street.

Exterior view
Carriage house

Wholesale Buildings, *Quincy.* 1871.

232   This grouping of commercial buildings (originally four,
       one was destroyed by fire in the late 1920's) was
       constructed for S. J. Lesem & Bros. Company (on the
       corner) and Kingsburg, Blasland & Co., manufacturers of
       boots and shoes. One building was used as a warehouse
       for S. J. Lesem & Bros. Here commerce achieved opulence,
       with cast-iron fronts and studied fenestration above.
       The buildings continue to be used for wholesale activity.

       The production of the structural cast-iron elements used
       in mid-nineteenth-century building marked the beginning
       of standardized metal skeletal construction. While this is
       our present historical viewpoint, contemporary advocates
       of cast iron regarded it principally as an expedient and
       prefabricated substitute for stone. In a pamphlet of 1858,
       John Bogardus (1800–1874), a successful producer of
       architectural cast iron, set forth its decided advantages:
       "Every style of architecture and every design the artist
       can conceive, however plain or however complicated,
       can be executed exactly in cast iron. . . ."

       "Fluted columns and Corinthian capitals, the most
       elaborate carvings, and the richest designs, which the
       architect may have dreamed of, but did not dare represent
       in his plans, may thus be reproduced for little more than
       the cost of ordinary castings. Ornamental architecture thus
       becomes practical, even with our limited means; and its
       general introduction would greatly tend to elevate the
       public taste for the beautiful, and to purify and gratify one
       of the finest qualities of the human mind."

       Address: 121, 127, 137 North Third Street.

General view of wholesale buildings
Detail of cast-iron columns

Huffman House, *Quincy. ca.* 1885.

234 Robust French Empire styling often asserted itself in
American Victorian buildings, as seen in the Huffman
House. Onto a relatively limited façade the designer has
crowded a variety of shapes, colors, and textures to delight
us. His brick and stone house is topped with a curved
mansard roof echoing the curved tower element. The
patterned slate of the roof and an ornamental iron
cresting finish off this lively design.

Its owner, M. F. Huffman, came to Quincy from Canada in
1866 and established a jewelry store which soon grew to
be, to quote a 1888 publication, "Without question the
most complete jewelry establishment anywhere in this
growing western country." It seems appropriate that a
prosperous jeweler should inhabit this rather grand,
albeit compact, house which echoes the design of the
reign of Napoleon III.

Address: 1469 Maine Street

Post Office, *Quincy*. 1887.

236   Quincy is a city of exceptional architectural variety and
quality. Styles ranging from Greek Revival to designs
influenced by Frank Lloyd Wright can be seen. Somewhat
unusual in style for Illinois is this post office building
prepared in Washington by the Supervising Architect of
the Treasury, Mifflin E. Bell (*ca.* 1846–1904). Its modified
early French Renaissance design is reminiscent of the
châteaux of the Loire Valley. The Hampshire Street
elevation is composed of a center arcaded portion
terminated by square pavilions. The prominent dormer
windows have sharply pointed gables, more animated than
the contrasting sedate composition below.

Address: Eighth and Hampshire Streets.

Old State Savings Loan and Trust Bank, *Quincy.*
1892 and 1906.

238   The high quality of this Romanesque-styled bank building
indicates that its unknown architect had considerable
ability, equal to that of John W. Root, Henry Cobb, or
Nathan Ricker. It is constructed of pink Missouri granite
with excellent carved ornamentation, and was certainly
among the finest buildings in the Midwest when occupied
in 1893. An addition to the bank was built in 1906,
designed by an architect named Ernest Wood. His extension on the right is in complete harmony with the original.

The bank was a continuation of the banking firm of
L. and C. H. Bull, established in 1861, which expanded
under the name of State Savings Loan and Trust Company.
Although no longer used as a bank, the structure is
fortunately to be preserved and used as a combination
office building, history museum, and cultural center.

Address: 428 Maine Street.

River Forest School, *River Forest*. 1860.

The responsibility the first arrivals in Illinois felt toward education and their eagerness to establish schools are documented in the many early communities of the state.

An example is this early schoolhouse in River Forest, which, though not the first in the village, was the largest and finest school building between Chicago and Elgin when it was completed in 1860. It was constructed by Ashbel Steele, an early merchant, sheriff, and contractor of the village, and its yard was planted with elms given by a school director, Solomon Thatcher. Known as Harlem School until 1879 when the school district was divided, one of its first teachers was Frances E. Willard. It served primarily as an eight-grade elementary school. In 1940 the building was remodeled for use as a school administration building.

The red brick walls, soft in color, are simply treated with pilaster strips and a corbelled moulding. Stone headings are used for the segmental and full arched windows. The cornices, pediment, and belfry are of wood. *HABS*.

Address: 7776 Lake Street at Park Avenue.

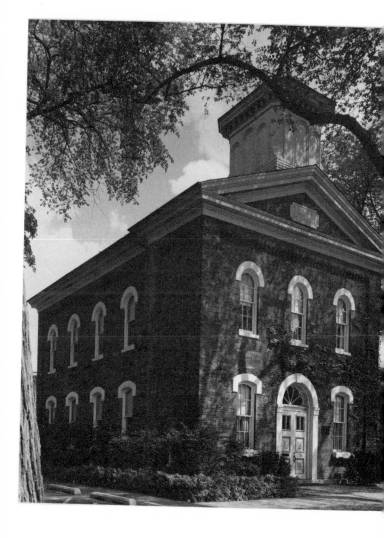

Winslow House, *River Forest.* 1893.

The William H. Winslow House is Frank Lloyd Wright's
first acknowledged independent work after leaving the
office of Adler and Sullivan. For six years he was the close
assistant of Louis Sullivan, and this experience was his only
substantial education in architecture. Although fiercely
independent, Wright freely proclaimed his debt to Sullivan.

Sullivan's influence in the facade is clearly seen in the
decorative band in cut stone around the doorway (a near
copy of the detail Sullivan used in the Wainwright Tomb
in St. Louis), the modeled plaster frieze of the second floor,
and the round-arched porte-cochere. Wright's contribution is seen in the affirmative low massing and the
importance of the sheltering roof. Here is the ancestor of
the prairie house. The rear elevation of the Winslow house
predicts Wright's future dynamism of forms: instead of
controlling the features within boxlike confines, as in the
front, Wright has expressed the stairway in a polygonal
tower and has projected the semicircular form of the
dining-room bay. This animation announces Wright's
independence.

The materials and colors used in this house are striking:
yellow-orange Tiffany brick surrounds the limestone center
portion; the frieze is painted dark brown; the roof was
originally of glazed bronze-colored tiles.

Equally noteworthy are the stables of wood construction
built the same year, whose cruciform composition
suggests, even more than the house itself, Wright's
future development. *HABS*.

Address: Auvergne Place.

River Forest Women's Club, *River Forest*. 1913.

244 The young draftsmen and architects who worked for Sullivan or Wright received more than a paycheck. They received the stimulus of a creative approach to design and an awareness of architecture's relation to life. When practicing independently, their designs continued the composition and ornament of their masters so that work of masters and followers alike can be called the "Prairie School" of architecture.

The River Forest Women's Club was one product of the five-year partnership of Louis Guenzel (1860–1956) and William E. Drummond (1876–1946). Both men had worked for Wright. Guenzel also had previous experience in the office of Adler and Sullivan. The Women's Club is a vigorous design executed in wood with horizontal board and batten siding. In composition it recalls Wright's earlier Unity Temple in adjacent Oak Park. A new entry and vestibule were added some years later but follow in the spirit of the original design.

Address: 526 Ashland Avenue.

Coonley House, *Riverside*. 1908.

246   Frank Lloyd Wright's compositional freedom is nowhere
better expressed than in his design for the Avery Coonley
House. He was fortunate in having a sympathetic client
and a generous site. He took advantage of the site in
extending the elements into an irregular U-shaped plan
which is not to be comprehended in a single glance.
Furthermore, all major rooms are on the second level so
one has a "balcony" view over surrounding lawns, pool,
and gardens. The total effect suggests the expansiveness
of a villa.

The house is of wood frame and stucco, rather unpromising
materials for a large house, but Wright has left us with a
particularly effective detail in the geometric frieze made of
colored square tiles pressed into the stucco. In a later
project for the Coonley estate, the Playhouse (1912),
Wright used bits of bright colored glass in the leaded
windows. In these geometrical colored patterns, Wright
anticipated the use of color abstraction in European
painting. The works of the Dutch *de Stijl* group and the
Russian Constructivist movement come to mind.

In conclusion, the Coonley House represents a master-
piece of Wright's early and fertile period, 1900–1913. It is
an enlarged version of the prairie house and has, like the
others, those curiously combined qualities of dynamism
and tranquility. *HABS*.

Address: 300 Scottswood Road.

Babson Service Buildings, *Riverside*. 1915–16.

248   Among the pupil-draftsmen who worked under Louis Sullivan, the most faithful and, next to Wright, the most talented was George Grant Elmslie (1871–1935). After many years of service Elmslie left Sullivan's employ in 1909 to form a partnership with William Gray Purcell (1880–1965) in Minneapolis. Purcell himself had had brief experience under Sullivan. The two architects had a flourishing practice in residential and bank buildings until their partnership ended in 1922.

The service buildings for Henry Babson were designed by Elmslie and complemented the Babson House designed by Louis Sullivan in 1908. The buildings are grouped around a service court and are properly more informal in character than the house. Indeed, in this particular design Elmslie's work is influenced more by Wright than by Sullivan. The decoration was done by Alfonso Iannelli (1888–1965), an architectural sculptor-designer who had worked with various architects of the Prairie School starting with Wright's Midway Gardens project in Chicago (1913). The service buildings were remodeled into residences in the 1930's and retain much of their original character. *HABS*.

Address: 283 Gatesby Road.

Herrick-Logli House, *Rockford.* 1849.

250 "Cobblestone houses" is the descriptive yet inaccurate term given to the rubble-walled houses common to parts of northern Illinois and southern Wisconsin whose surface is set with meticulous horizontal rows of small stones. Cobblestones proper measure six to twelve inches in diameter whereas these houses use small, undressed stones from the river banks. In this example in Rockford, stones from the Rock River were gathered with the black ones being reserved for the front of the house. Limestone quoins are used at the corners, and wood is used for the lintels and sills. In general outline the house is a derivative of the Greek Revival.

There is little documentation as to the origin of this type of construction. It is thought to derive from the cobblestone houses seen in New York State. *HABS.*

Address: 2127 Broadway.

Lake-Peterson House, *Rockford*. 1873.

The Gothic Revival began in mid-eighteenth-century England when amateur architect and author Horace Walpole remodeled his estate, Strawberry Hill, in Twickenham. The result was a fanciful Gothic design more visually effective than historically accurate. The pleasure Walpole received from his scenic Gothic efforts reinforced his Romantic literary tastes and satisfied his dilettante curiosity.

Much of this fanciful Gothic styling was carried into the nineteenth century. An excellent example is the Lake-Peterson House. It is constructed of yellow brick and ornamented with porches, tracery bargeboards, and decorative gables. Its original owner was John H. Lake, an Englishman who settled in Rockford in 1837 and became a prominent lumber dealer and contractor. The house was kept in the Lake family until 1918 when it was sold to Pehr A. Peterson. Swedish-born Peterson was a successful business man whose community efforts included the development of the Swedish-American Hospital. The hospital now uses the Peterson home as a residence for student nurses.

Address: 1313 East State Street.

Davenport House, *Rock Island*. 1833.

254   The builder of this house was Colonel George Davenport,
a trader who enjoyed great prestige among the Indians
and white settlers of the region. He laid out the town of
Davenport, Iowa, and took part in negotiating the treaty of
1842 with the Sacs and Foxes. He was a man of broad
culture who traveled widely through the East and the
South. Born in England in 1783, Davenport came up the
Mississippi in 1816. He was killed by river ruffians in
1845 on his own threshold.

The house is of advanced design for that period in Illinois.
Originally it had flanking one-story wings which presented
a broad elevation facing the Mississippi. The house was
rebuilt in 1906 without these wings or a third, rear, service
wing. The plan of the main block iş only one room deep.
Wood frame construction with clapboards and fieldstone
chimneys are used. Among the fine details are a fanlighted
doorway, a columnar portico, and tin conductor heads
ornamented with the date and embossed stars. *HABS*.

Address: Rock Island Arsenal Grounds.

Exterior view today
Restored elevation drawing

Mack House, *Rockton*. 1839.

Stephen Mack was the first permanent white settler in
Winnebago County and a descendent of John Mack, a
Scot who settled in Connecticut in 1669. Mack established
a trading post at Grand Detour in 1824. While in this village
Mack married an Indian girl, Hononegah. In 1829 he left
Grand Detour and came to live with the Winnebago
Indians at Bird's Grove, where he established a trading
post. Bird's Grove is now Hononegah Park.

In 1835 he established Macktown on the south bank of the
Pecatonica River near where it joins the Rock River. His
large tract of land was partly plotted and lots were sold.
Mack's settlement was not destined to flourish long; after
his death in 1850 the community deteriorated and nothing
is known of the village plan.

One of the three surviving buildings of Macktown is the
two-story house which Stephen Mack built for himself in
1839, an ambitious house for its time and place—said to be
the first two-storied painted house west of Chicago. It is
constructed of heavy timber frame with clapboard siding.
Its design is faintly neoclassical in outline and detail. In
1956 the house was opened as a museum and home of
the Rockton Township Historical Society.

A second surviving building is the nearby Whitman's
Trading Post, built in 1846. This building, consisting of four
small connected units, is built of native limestone, a
characteristic building material of the area.

Address: Winnebago County Forest Preserve.

Mack House
Whitman's Trading Post

Talcott-Olson House, *Rockton*. 1843.

Like Stephen Mack who settled across the Pecatonica River, Captain William Talcott, the founder of Rockton, was a descendant of early American settlers. His ancestor was John Talcott, who came to the New World in 1632 and was the founder of Hartford, Connecticut. Captain Talcott and his oldest son Thomas were exploring the area along Rock River for possible settlement in 1835 and met up with Stephen Mack who had recently made a claim near the junction of the Pecatonica and Rock rivers. Father and son staked their claim on the opposite bank. In a few years they had built a millrace across the big bend in the Rock River, provided power for a sawmill and gristmill, and assured prosperity and stability for their new settlement of Pecatonic, renamed Rockton in 1844.

Among the half-hundred stone houses and buildings extant in Rockton is the house of Walter Henry Talcott, another of Captain Talcott's sons. The front portion is two and one-half stories, with a west wing of a story and a half. The gable ends project above the roof to form a parapet and originally had a pair of immense stone chimneys. Their removal long ago has been a loss to the design. At one time a porch was built across the house, probably a later addition. The present porch is of recent date and inappropriate. The doorway deserves special mention: it is entirely of wood, rather ornate in concept, but naïve in execution. The side lights are ornamented with a carved vine-like design. Above is the transom with a carved design suggesting an attenuated anthemion, a favorite classical motif.

Address: 302 Blackhawk Boulevard.

Front doorway detail
Exterior view

Old Stone Church, *Rockton*, 1848–50.

260   This building, also known as the First Congregational Church, combines native limestone walls, commonly seen in Rockton, with the simple monumentality of the neoclassic style. Four pilaster strips are worked into the masonry façade and two wood Doric columns are recessed within a shallow porch. The entablature and pediment are of wood as well. A belfry and steeple, a recent replacement of an earlier one blown down in 1913, complete the design. Records tell us that a John Peterson was the designer of this church. The congregation was organized in 1838, largely through the efforts of the Talcott family which founded Rockton. *HABS.*

Address: Blackhawk Boulevard and East Union Street.

Half-Way House, *Salem.* ca. 1820.

About halfway on the westward Vincennes–St. Louis trail a southwestern trail to Kaskaskia branched off. At the juncture of these two early overland routes stood a tavern known to have existed in 1779 when George Rogers Clark and his troops came through on their way to take the fort at Vincennes. The present inn stands on the same site and was built in the 1820's by John Middleton. Before the railroads this was a stage stop for regularly scheduled cross-country coaches connecting the two river cities to Vincennes.

The Half-Way House had good accommodations for the traveler and his horses and for stagecoaches and their passengers. It was a commodious outlay of buildings of which only one two-story unit remains, and that in poor condition. It is being restored to its original condition in which three additional two-story houses were joined to the present one, forming an extended group about seventy feet long. Long porches on both floor levels are known to have existed, presenting a somewhat impressive appearance.

The Half-Way House is built of oak logs notched and fitted at the corners; much of the chinking and daubing used to fill spaces between the logs remains. The siding was made by splitting oak into clapboards about four feet long and applying them as weatherboarding, much of which also remains.

Old Orchard Shopping Center, *Skokie*. 1954.

264   The expansion of the suburbs of larger cities after World
        War II brought about a new development in shopping
        habits which is now an accepted part of the American
        scene, the shopping center. These centers have challenged
        the importance of the traditional downtown cluster of
        stores.

        Most shopping centers are designed and built without
        architectural distinction. An exception is Old Orchard,
        designed by Loebl, Schlossman, and Bennett. The land-
        scape architect was Lawrence Halprin. Much of the
        success of this center is due to the attractive landscaped
        pedestrian malls which are created by the arrangement of
        buildings. The materials used are rough hewn stone, white
        brick, and copper roofing. These choices, together with
        the landscaping, attempt to harmonize the shopping center
        with its suburban setting. Much attention was given to
        lighting effects because the biggest volume of business is
        done at night. A standard of design regarding signs
        prevented the senseless competition and visual chaos
        common to unplanned business districts.

Address: Old Orchard Road and Skokie Highway.

Charter Oak School, *Sparta*. 1873.

Although Orson Squire Fowler (1809–87) was not primarily an architect, it was he who established the popularity for octagonal buildings in the second half of the nineteenth century. By profession he was a successful lecturer and writer on diverse subjects: phrenology, the abolition of slavery, temperance, and practical building. Fowler believed the octagonal plan to be "cheap, convenient and superior," and favored its use for houses, churches, schools, and other buildings. He set forth his functional ideas in a book entitled, *A Home for All,* published in 1853, and he himself lived contentedly, we assume, in an octagonal house in Fishkill, New York.

Fowler's practicality and persuasiveness of argument probably influenced Daniel Ling, an easterner and teacher during the school year 1872–73, to propose this contro- versial octagonal plan for the new one-room schoolhouse at Schuline, near Sparta. Seats were arranged on five sides, with radial aisles, and every pupil could easily be supervised by the teacher. Windows on seven of the sides provided equal light. Blackboard space was ample. Fowler also suggested that the octagonal shape was less vulnerable to windstorms. The cost of this rural schoolhouse was $1,000. In 1883 a bell was purchased and a belfrey built.

This unusual schoolhouse is the only one of its kind in Illinois and one of three in the United States. It was in use until 1953 when a new consolidated school was opened. It is now owned by the Randolph County Historical Society.

Address: Schuline, two miles south of Sparta on Ill. 4.

Edwards Place, *Springfield*. 1833 and ca. 1855.

268   The Edwards Place was originally a one and one-half story
      frame house erected in 1833 by a Dr. Thomas Houghan.
      It is the oldest house on its own grounds in Springfield and
      once stood on its own fourteen-acre site outside the
      city limits.

      In 1843 it was purchased by Benjamin S. Edwards, son of
      Ninian Edwards, first territorial governor and afterwards
      third state governor of Illinois. In the 1850's a large brick
      portion was added in front of the original house, a design
      based on one suggested in an architectural handbook
      published in 1852, Samuel Sloan's *The Model Architect*.
      The extremely wide eaves, intended for a house in the
      South, are supported by large spaced and paired brackets.
      The hip roof which supplanted the gable roof at this time
      is surmounted by a low square cupola. Across the front
      stretches a handsome Corinthian porch. Many details
      accurately follow Sloan's printed design.

      In 1913 the house was given to the Springfield Art Study
      Club and is now the Springfield Art Association. A side
      picture gallery conforming to the architecture of the
      house was added in 1937–38.

      Address: 700 North Fourth Street.

Old State Capitol, *Springfield*. 1837.

Starting with the Capitol in Washington, the dome became the symbol of government buildings of all sorts throughout the nineteenth century. In the 1830's the Classical Revival reached its crest, and for the new Illinois State Capitol the architect, John Francis Rague (1799–1877), followed the formula established by the architects Town and Davis in their designs for the North Carolina and Indiana Capitols: the combination of a Roman inspired dome with a Greek Doric portico. In 1849 the dome was rebuilt on a modified design. In 1899–1901 the building was raised and a full basement story inserted. Raising the building eleven feet on jacks in twelve days was considered the engineering feat of all time. The building had become the Sangamon County Courthouse by 1876 when the new and present capitol was ready for occupancy.

The old capitol was rebuilt in 1966–68 to conform to its original appearance, re-using the exterior stones, but with a new inner structure. It now serves as a historic shrine. In the Hall of Representatives, Abraham Lincoln and Stephen A. Douglas debated questions of state, and the former delivered, on the occasion of his nomination to the U. S. Senate in June, 1858, the memorable speech in which he said, "A house divided against itself cannot stand. I believe this government cannot endure, permanently half *slave* and half *free*." *HABS*.

Address: Adams Street between Fifth and Sixth Streets.

Lincoln Home, *Springfield,* 1839 and 1856.

One of the most popular historic sites in America is Abraham Lincoln's Springfield home, where he lived for seventeen years, leaving it in 1861 for the White House. It was donated to the state in 1887 by Robert Todd Lincoln. Between 1950 and 1955 the house was accurately restored and furnished to resemble its appearance in about 1860.

In January, 1844, Lincoln purchased the house from the Rev. Charles Dresser who had officiated at his marriage to Mary Todd fourteen months earlier. The house was built in 1839 of simplified Greek Revival design, a story and a half in front, one story at the rear. To accommodate their family of three sons, the Lincolns enlarged the house in 1856, creating the full two-story house, front and back, that we see today.

Careful research has authenticated all details of restoration, from the light brown exterior color to the carriage house, woodshed, and privy in the backyard. In his remodeling, Lincoln enlarged the front parlor into a double one divided by folding doors. Sketches of the double parlor and the sitting room which appeared in *Leslie's Illustrated Weekly* on March 9, 1861, were invaluable in determining the original appearance of these rooms. They are, "as the reader may observe, simply and plainly fitted up, but are not without indications of taste and refinement. . . . The rooms are elegantly and comfortably furnished with strong well-made furniture, made for use and not for show."

Address: Eighth and Jackson Streets.

274   This is the first and only building erected by the state as the official residence for the governor and his family. For some years after the move of the capital to Springfield (1839), the governors lived in a nearby modest brick house owned by the state. In 1853 the legislature appropriated funds for a proper mansion, which was completed in November, 1855, and first occupied by Governor Joel A. Matteson and his family.

The architect of the Executive Mansion was John Murray Van Osdel (1811–91). He left New York for Chicago in 1837 and had a long and distinguished career in that city designing important homes, hotels, and commercial buildings both before and after the 1871 fire. Van Osdel was also the architect of University Hall, the first building on the University of Illinois campus.

The original design for the Executive Mansion illustrated the changeover from classical influence to early Victorian style. It is constructed of red pressed brick (now painted) manufactured in Springfield. Before alterations it had a low roof, lower pediment, and a splendid glazed cupola twenty-eight feet in height from the cornice of the building, which gave light into a central circular stair. Van Osdel arranged around a central hall seven large rooms which opened into each other by means of sliding doors, so that when all were open a promenade was formed of the entire first story. About 1889 remodeling altered the nature of Van Osdel's design: the roof was raised, the cupola removed, a balustrade substituted, and white paint applied.

Address: Jackson Street between Fourth and Fifth Streets.

Present view
Original design of the Executive Mansion

State Capitol, *Springfield*. 1868–88.

This is the fifth state capitol building of Illinois. In March, 1867, a competition for the design of a new capitol was announced with a prize of $3,000. About twenty-one entries were received from architects in various states, among them John Van Osdel of Chicago and Alexander Jackson Davis of New York. The winner was John Crombie Cochrane (1833–87) of Chicago. His partner, Alfred H. Piquenard (? –1876), was partially responsible for this building.

The legislature had originally limited the cost of the new capitol to $3,000,000, but the amount was increased by the Constitution of 1870 to $3,500,000. Although incomplete, the building was occupied in 1874. In 1877 and again in 1882 voters refused an approval of appropriations to complete the building. However this was done in 1884 and the capitol was declared completed in 1888 at a cost of $4,500,000, twenty years after it was begun.

The new capitol provided for Senate and Representative chambers in the north and south wings respectively and the Supreme Court and law library in the west wing. Precedent of a central rotunda with dome separating two legislative wings was established with Dr. Thornton's plan for the U. S. Capitol. "The convenience and capacity of the new State House," read the Legislative Handbook of 1877, "in contrast with the old one, is like moving from a hovel to a palace."

Speaking of his own design, architect Cochrane wrote, "In the plans presented, it will be observed that many objections common to our public buildings, have been avoided; and superior improvements incorporated. Likewise all unnecessary and useless ornament has been discarded, and yet no mechanical exigencies permitted to subordinate the artistic."

Dana House, *Springfield.* 1904.

278 The richness and satisfying complexity of architecture was exploited by Frank Lloyd Wright in several commissions which allowed him free reign. Such an example is the Susan Lawrence Dana House, which replaced the old Rheuna Drake Lawrence House, where the heiress of Colorado silver mines was born.

In this design Wright has assembled all those experiments he had previously tried: the cruciform plan, the connecting galleries, the curved vaulted ceilings, the sloping roofs, and the bold horizontal lines combined with powerful vertical piers. Mrs. Dana also allowed him to design all the interior fittings, furniture, and decoration, which he was happy to do. The leaded-glass casement windows, a specialty of Wright's early work, are magnificent.

Address: 301 Lawrence Avenue.

Dr. Hall's Office, *Toulon.* 1848-49.

280   Dr. Thomas Hall, English born and trained in his profession, came to Toulon from nearby Osceola in 1842. He wanted a separate office building for his practice and, though he preferred a Gothic design, his son, an attorney and architect, prepared the details for this decorative miniature temple. It is only 14 feet by 18 feet. Dr. Hall maintained his own pharmacy in the outer office. The building has been restored, some of the portico details inaccurately. It was once common for lawyers and doctors to build detached offices for their practice. Dr. Hall's office is one of a few such structures remaining in Illinois. *HABS.*

Address: Franklin Street.

Altgeld Hall, University of Illinois, *Urbana*. 1896.

In 1862 Congress passed the Morrill Act which provided for land-grant colleges and resulted in the 1867 charter for Illinois Industrial College, later to become the University of Illinois. Its educational role was undefined in its early years, and not until Governor John Altgeld's term (1892–96) did it expand and prosper. When Altgeld became governor the university occupied four old buildings and had a faculty of forty-eight. At the end of his term six new buildings had been provided and the faculty increased to one hundred and seventy.

One of the new buildings was the university library, now Altgeld Hall. It was designed by Professor Nathan C. Ricker (1843–1924), who was then head of the department of architecture as well as dean of the college of engineering, and James M. White of the department of architecture. The masonry is quarry-faced Minnesota sandstone, with which the architects achieved massive lintels, functioning arches, and deep reveals of shadow characteristic of the Richardsonian Romanesque manner. They also incorporated reinforced concrete in the floor and roof construction, making the building highly fire resistant. The interior scheme of decoration employs mosaics and is Byzantine in inspiration and form.

Christian Science Student Center, *Urbana*. 1956.

284 The early lessons of modern architecture emphasized a
regularity and simplicity of plan and elevation. Sculptural
forms and irregular silhouettes were considered arbitrary
and inappropriate, as well as being associated with
historical revival styling. These dicta were challenged by a
second generation of modern architects. Schooled in
Bauhaus principles, they rejected them as too narrow,
limiting the range of architectural expression. By the 1960's
this reaction was apparent in many designs which proved
just as puzzling to the public as were the earlier pioneer
modern designs.

Such an example is Paul Rudolph's (1918–   ) Christian
Science Student Center. A small building with an aggressive
air, it is neither bland nor inconspicuous, but speaks out
in favor of individuality and complexity. Different volumes,
textures, and colors help to achieve this effect. The ceilings
range from seven feet four inches to forty-two feet high
which creates an illusion of either great size or intimacy
depending on the number of occupants. Sliding panels
convert spaces into large or small areas. The exterior
texture, striated concrete with exposed aggregate, gives an
effect that is raw and vigorous. The opaque tower forms
suggest a medieval fortress but without any direct allusion.

The sculptural bronze doors are the work of
Roger Majorowicz.

Address: Fourth Street and Gregory Drive.

Vandalia State House, *Vandalia*. 1836.

286   The first General Assembly of Illinois met October 5, 1818, in rented rooms in Kaskaskia, the first capital. It was intended to choose another site more centrally located. Vandalia was subsequently chosen and declared the capital for the next twenty years. A very simple wood statehouse was built in 1820 but burned in 1823. In the summer of 1824 the citizens of Vandalia, without legislative authorization, remodeled the shell of a burned-out brick bank building which was accepted as the second statehouse and used until 1836.

Agitation for moving the capital farther northward in the early 1830's was counteracted by the efforts of the townspeople to hold the state capital at Vandalia. In the summer of 1836 they acted again without legislative authority, tore down the second statehouse, and hurriedly built a new and third one. It was destined to serve only two years. In February, 1839, the building was given to Fayette County and the town of Vandalia.

Plans for the third statehouse were prepared by John Taylor and William Hodge. It was embellished only with a small wood cupola. Material from the second statehouse was used as far as possible in building the third. In 1858–59 brick porticoes were added to the north and south façades, and later replaced with cast-iron columns in 1899. The brick porticoes were rebuilt when the former statehouse was restored in 1933–39 as a historic Illinois building.

Address: 315 West Gallatin Street.

Swartout House, *Waukegan.* 1847.

In the spread of the Greek Revival, knowledge of classical motifs was transmitted by architectural handbooks which were commonly used by carpenters. Among popular authors were Asher Benjamin, Minard Lafever, and Edward Shaw. Their handbooks often bore descriptive titles such as *Young Builder's General Instructor* and *Practical House Carpenter*. These books contained simple advice and many illustrations to guide the carpenter-architect. Needless to say, he often took liberties with the classical details.

This small temple-fronted house might as well have been built in Michigan or Ohio as in Illinois. Originally it was truly diminutive; a large rear portion was added in 1858, the north bay window in 1877, and the south porch enclosed in 1933. Architectural sophistication is concentrated at the portico front: Doric columns, fretted pilaster strips, and eared window frames, all of which were doubtlessly lifted from a builder's pocket guide. The original owner was John H. Swartout. *HABS.*

Address: 414 Sheridan Road.

Lake County Tuberculosis Sanatorium, *Waukegan*.
1939.

290   During the 1930's America received the liberating
influence of new architectural ideas from Europe. In
Germany and Holland, in particular, an architectural style
had crystallized which was intended to express the long
neglected structural and functional aspects of architecture.
Aesthetically the new architecture was characterized by
transparency and abstraction of planes. It avoided
ornament altogether. It was recognized that the
requirements of contemporary buildings were
incompatible with the façades of classical, Gothic, or
Georgian designs.

The embodiment of this European development was the
German *Bauhaus* founded by Walter Gropius in 1919.
After the breakup of this school in 1934, many of its
teachers emigrated to America, among them Mies van der
Rohe and Moholy-Nagy who came to Chicago. Gradually
American architectural schools were reorganized after
the *Bauhaus* curriculum.

An early and successful example of this new architecture
is the Lake County Tuberculosis Sanatorium designed by
William A. Ganster (1908–   ) and William L. Pereira
(1910–   ). Here the requirements of tuberculosis
patients and the maintenance of a sanatorium are reflected
in the architect's design. The bedrooms are lined up facing
south and opening directly onto a continuous balcony
for the daytime use of patients. On the north are placed
the administrative and medical facilities. The sanatorium is
beautifully sited in a partly wooded landscape. Every
aspect of its design is carefully thought out to achieve
those therapeutic benefits which good architecture and
nature can provide.

Address: 2400 Belvidere Street.

St. Anastasia's Church, *Waukegan*. 1964.

292   The plan of St. Anastasia's Church is a simple rectangle with a wide chancel across the front and a balcony over the back portion. The architects, I. W. Colburn (1924-   ) and Associates, have enriched this essentially boxlike form with two motifs, the arch and the perforated wall, both executed in red brick. The arch motif is developed into a series of domed canopies which are used processionally within and without the flanking walls. Two larger versions of this form are extended above the flat roof and suggest open belfry towers. Three smaller domed canopies are linked to form an entrance portico.

The second motif is the perforated wall in which colored glass is set within a textured brick surface. The glass is scarcely visible from the exterior, but inside jewel-like colors glow and relieve the monochromatic brick interior. Dramatic skylighting is the major source of daylight. The combination of simplicity and richness, of variety and limited architectural motifs, makes the design of this church exceptional.

Address: 624 Douglas Avenue.

Entrance to the church
Interior view toward altar

Bahá'i House of Worship, *Wilmette*. 1920–21, 1930–43, 1947–52.

This House of Worship was built by members of the Bahá'i Faith, an independent world religion which originated in Persia in 1844. The Bahá'i Faith centers on three principles: the oneness of God, the oneness of religion, and the oneness of mankind.

A nine-sided building was prescribed. A French-Canadian architect, Louis J. Bourgeois (1856–1930), prepared a design which, while seemingly Near Eastern in character, is a blending of many architectural forms. The structure consists of a ninety-foot in diameter circular dome and clerestory whose ribs are carried on nine columns of a polygonal drum. The base portion and drum are unaligned but are similarly treated with filigree ornament on their concave surfaces. The sculptor for this ornamentation was John J. Earley. The structure proper is of reinforced concrete with exterior panels and window grilles cast in a combination of white cement, ground quartz, and white granite aggregate. The radiant quality of this material is highly appropriate to the exotic and elegant design.

Address: 112 Linden Avenue.

Crow Island Elementary School, *Winnetka*. 1939–40.

296   The capacity of architecture to bring spirit into our lives,
      to sustain a sympathetic environment, has too often been
      neglected in school buildings. This progressive school is
      exemplary as an architectural expression of an educational
      philosophy. The school as a place for learning, making, and
      doing has been intelligently and sympathetically expressed
      by the architects Eliel and Eero Saarinen and Perkins,
      Wheeler, and Will. Credit for its success is also due to
      the local school officials.

      The stubborn box common to traditional school buildings
      has been discarded in favor of a center block with three
      expansive wings (a fourth wing was added in 1954) so that
      various activities and age groups are identified archi-
      tecturally. Classrooms have simple furniture fitted to the
      sizes of children, and each has its own lavatory, sink, and
      drinking fountain. A work alcove is provided for special
      class projects and each classroom has its own private exit
      and courtyard. When the school was built, such con-
      siderations were not common in school design and the
      building itself was an educational experience for other
      architects, educators, and the public. Eliel Saarinen (1873–
      1950) was born in Finland and established a practice in this
      country in the 1920's and later was assisted by his son,
      Eero. Both father and son have been the architects of
      many distinguished buildings.

      Address: Willow Road.

Union Tank Car Company Dome, *Wood River*. 1961.

298   A unique figure in American architecture is R. Buckminster
Fuller (1895–   ). Neither his approach nor his results
fall within the conventions of architecture. Fuller has
combined the knowledge of various sciences, engineering,
and mathematics with an application amounting to a
personal invention of a new structural system. The
originality and efficiency of his domed structures have
amazed and confounded both professionals and laymen.

Fuller's executed domes have been of varying sizes and
materials and have been used for diverse purposes. His
United States Pavilion for the 1967 Montreal World's Fair
is one example. In Wood River stands one of two similar
domes he has designed for the Union Tank Car Company
for use as repair and maintenance shops for railroad tank
cars. The span is 384 feet, the height is 120 feet at center.
The dome covers an area of two and one-half acres of
unencumbered space. It is constructed of folded eighth-
inch-thick sheet steel in hexagonal panels with pipe
connections and tension rods. The depth of this trusslike
membering is four feet. The parts are simple in shape and
few in type. The assembled dome bears a proportional
structural weight of only two ounces for each cubic foot
of enclosure.

Opera House, *Woodstock*. 1889.

300   This building was a city venture voted in 1889 with the
      mayor casting the deciding vote when the city council was
      tied on the matter. It was designed to serve as a city hall,
      public library, and theater as well. The long and varied
      history of this theater has included both amateur and
      professional productions. In 1961 the Woodstock Fine Arts
      Association was formed to provide a necessary continuing
      organization for greater activity including workshop
      courses, student productions, and films.

Address: Dean and Van Buren Streets.

Index

Index